CONTENTS

First published in Great Britain in 1996
by Hamlyn, an imprint of Reed Consumer Books Limited
Michelin House, 81 Fulham Road, London SW3 6RB
and Auckland, Melbourne, Singapore and Toronto

Copyright © 1996 Reed International Books Limited

ISBN 0 600 58991 9

A catalogue record for this book is available from the British Library

Produced by Mandarin Offset
Printed in Hong Kong

▶▶

Brad Pitt

AN ILLUSTRATED STORY

CAROLINE WESTBROOK

HAMLYN

Author's Acknowledgments
The author would like to thank the following for their assistance and support:
Julian Brown, Leslie Bunder, Helen and David Westbrook, Ian 'Just Married' Westbrook, Hugh Westbrook, Pamela Melnikoff. And a special big thank you to Good Ghost (we all have imaginary friends . . .)

Photographic Acknowledgements
Front cover: **Aquarius Picture Library**
Back cover top: **All Action**/Alban
bottom, left to right: **All Action**/Jean Cummings, **Ronald Grant Archive, Pictorial Press.**
All Action 5 centre top, 5 bottom centre, 12 left, 14/15, 27, 28/9, 43 top, 52 top, 60/1, 77 centre, 13, 19 top right, /Dave Hogan 21.
Aquarius Picture Library 5 centre left, 10, 32/3, 35, 40/1, 51 bottom right, 58 bottom, 62/3, 64/5, 68 bottom left, 69 top right, 77 right, 77 left, 79, /Philip Caruso 73 top right.
Corbis/Bettmann/ Everett 5 botttom right, 5 bottom left, 5 centre right, 18, 20, 25 top right, 31 bottom right, 31 top right, 41 top right, 44, 46/7, 49, 50/1, 54/5, 56/7, 58 top, 67, 68/9, 70/1, 73 bottom right, 76 left, 78 right, 78 left .
Ronald Grant Archive 11 top right, 26 bottom left, 42, 45 top right, 57 bottom, 66, 68 centre left, 69 top left, 76 right.
Katz 2/3, 11 bottom right, 17 bottom right, 36 top left, 48 bottom left, 53, /Steve Sands 19 bottom right.
Photofest 36/7, 78 centre.
Pictorial Press 5 centre, 9, 12 centre, 24/5, 26 top left, 34, 38/9, 41 bottom right, 45 left, 48 centre left, 48 top left, 51 top right, 57 top, 59, /William Rutten 17 top right.
Retna 11 centre right, 25 bottom right, 30, /Fitzroy Barrett 45 bottom right, /Michael Benabib 5 top left, 6/7, /Bill Davila 74 bottom left, 74 top left, /Steve Granitz 36 bottom left, /Photofest 5 top right, 22/23.
Rex Features 8 top, 12 right, 43 right, 52 bottom left, 63, 69 bottom right, 72, 75, /Cesare Bonazza 16, /Richard Young 80.

Executive Editor Julian Brown
Assistant Editor Karen O'Grady
Production Controller Melanie Frantz
Picture Research Wendy Gay
Design Steve Byrne

1 BRINGING UP BRAD

Bringing Up Brad

Above: Brad Pitt hides from the limelight with his fiancee, actress Gwyneth Paltrow

Opposite: Brad's matinee idol good looks have spawned a female following from all over the world

From humble beginnings to Hollywood success

In just five years, Brad Pitt has gone from being a penniless would-be actor donning a chicken costume for a living, to one of the most recognisable faces in 90s cinema, a renowned heart-throb who can not only pocket around eight million dollars just to show his face on screen but is also blessed with the uncanny ability to be able to act.

Like his peers Keanu Reeves and Johnny Depp, Brad's matinee idol good looks have spawned him a female following the world over, while those more closely involved in the business of making movies have likened him to such legends as James Dean or Robert Redford.

William Bradley Pitt was born on December 18, 1963 in Shawnee, Oklahoma, to Baptist couple William (Bill) and Jane Pitt, and was the eldest of three children. However, he had very little contact with his tiny place of birth, as his father, manager of a trucking company, landed a new job while

his eldest son was still a baby, meaning that the three of them had to up and move to Springfield, Missouri (home of one of TV's most famous fictional families, *The Simpsons*). It was there that two further arrivals were welcomed into the family; younger son Douglas and sister Julie, who both made their appearance by the time Brad, known by his middle name since birth to differentiate from his father, was five.

Bill Pitt's new, more executive position meant he was away on business trips a lot, but he compensated by taking his children on the road with him whenever their school holidays coincided with a trip. It was this, more than anything, that emphasised just how close-knit the family were – and indeed, still are to this day, with Brad returning to the family fold whenever possible. Even today his humble beginnings are glaringly obvious; with his laid-back, relaxed, persona, Brad has cemented a reputation as one of the

most likable, easy-going young actors working in Hollywood.

Religion was a key part of Brad's formative years, and by the age of six he had already joined the choir of the South Haven Baptist Church in his home town, which even at such an early age attracted him more than his fair share of attention – his blond locks, blue eyes and expressive face made him stand out from the crowd.

It was at this time in his life that he discovered movies, having been taken to the local drive-in by his parents to see the 1969 Paul Newman/Robert Redford classic *Butch Cassidy and the Sundance Kid.* However, his first experience of cinema pretty much passed over his six-year-old head unnoticed. It wasn't until he saw The Who's rock musical *Tommy* in 1975 that he realised the effect that a piece of movie-making could have on him – he made a return trip to the cinema purely to see Elton John's Pinball Wizard sequence a second time.

In fact, it was Elton who introduced him to the world of rock music. Again, while music was something he had grown up hearing but never actually properly listened to (with the exception of the religious songs he sang in the church choir), his first encounter with Elton's classic ballad 'Daniel' changed all that. From that day on, Brad scraped together his pocket money until he could afford to buy Elton's Captain Fantastic album (on which the song was featured) which he played constantly and memorised, even going so far as to quote lines from Elton's songs in conversation. The music prompted him to learn the guitar, nurturing in his head the still unrealized ambition of belting out rock music for a living.

The film which had a similar effect on Brad's life was the Charlton Heston starrer *Planet of the Apes.* Again, having been shipped off to the drive-in by his parents, Brad never forgot the experience, still listing the finale, in which the Statue of Liberty is discovered buried in sand, as one of his all-time favourite movie moments.

However, the acting bug failed to bite in the same way as music. At Kickapoo High School, where Brad spent his teenage years, he willingly participated in school plays but never quite graduated to lead roles. This probably had much to do with the way in which he threw himself willingly into every activity. A bright, attentive student, something which stemmed from his parents' constant encouragement, Brad was into everything, including the student council, the debating society, singing, art – he often carried a notepad and pencil about his person should the urge to sketch something crop up – and, most notably, baseball. The scar on his left cheekbone is testament to his love of the latter – while fielding during one game, the sun caused him to lose sight of the ball which subsequently whacked him in the face. However, Brad recalls proudly that he still managed to out the batter, despite blood pouring down his face.

Then, of course, there was the small matter of the opposite sex, something Brad discovered while he was in fourth grade. His first girlfriend was Kim Bell, whom he met in junior high school, although by the time he reached senior school he was one of the most popular students among his fellow female academics, thanks to both his good looks and sparkling, vibrant personality. But, he spurned their advances because of steady girlfriend Sara Hart, whom he met when she was on the opposing side of an inter-school debate that he attended. The next day, in order to attract her attention, he went over to her high school and charmed her into submission by writing her name in the snow outside her classroom window.

Their first date was on Valentine's Day, when the pair went out to dinner and then home to meet Brad's parents. From then on, they appeared to be so inseparable that some thought they would be together for ever. Sadly, having been to each other's high school proms together, both of which took place on the same night, the two went their separate ways as college beckoned.

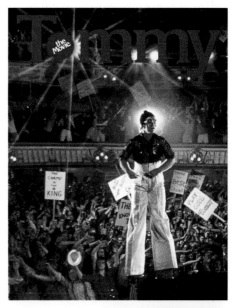

Top and *above:* The Who's *Tommy,* and Charlton Heston in *Planet of the Apes* – the movies that changed Brad's life

Below: Brad as an earnest young man

▶▶

Bringing Up Brad

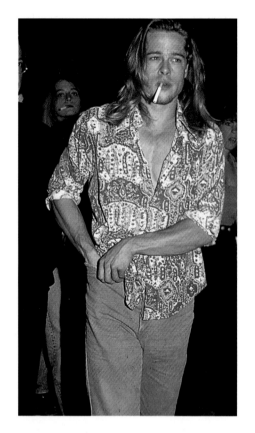

Above: The long-haired *Interview With the Vampire* look

Above centre: Brad in his grungy *Kaliforния* period

Above right: How Brad looks today – the cropped hair of *Seven*

Opposite: Brad again with long hair for *Legends of the Fall*

At the age of 17, Brad left home for the first time, to attend the University of Missouri, where he majored in journalism, despite harbouring aspirations to become an advertising art director, a profession which would utilise his interests in both writing and design.

Feeling free of family ties for the first time, Brad joined a college fraternity known as Sigma Chi, and became something of a party animal together with his new-found chums. He unsurprisingly became something of a campus heart-throb, a reputation garnered after he posed bare-chested for a fund-raising university calendar. However, it was also a time of reflection, not only causing him to reject the religion that had been such an integral part of his upbringing, but also to query his choice of a future career. It was sparked off by a nearly tragic accident in 1986, in which Brad's Buick, a family heirloom that he had inherited from his father upon passing his driving test, was written off

by a truck. Miraculously, Brad and the passengers travelling with him escaped without a scratch. But it was soon after that that Brad wanted to achieve more than was mapped out for him – a cosy executive job in advertising, with the inevitable marriage and children somewhere down the line, all contained within the Missouri setting where he had lived his life to date.

Brad decided he wanted more and, without further ado, decided to pack up his silver Datsun and head for Los Angeles to try his luck in the acting profession. After all, movies had already been an integral part of his life. Just two weeks before graduation, one exam paper short of securing his degree, and giving his parents no indication of what he was planning to do, Brad headed for Hollywood with just a handful of Stevie Ray Vaughan cassettes, his belongings and $325 in his pocket. He had no idea just what the future would hold. And, for the time being that was just the way he liked it.

2

FILMS, FAME AND FAST FOOD

Brad with *Dallas* co-star Shalane MacCall

Brad becomes one of the top stars of 90's cinema

Brad's first image of Los Angeles was not exactly the glittering film star haven that he had imagined. Arriving in Burbank, through a smog so thick that a person could almost hold on to it, he stopped at a McDonalds, and couldn't help wondering whether there shouldn't be more to L.A. than he had so far witnessed.

At this stage, he hadn't mentioned his crazy scheme to his parents, having instead told them that he was heading for the West Coast to study graphic design at Pasedena's Art Center College of Design. This, however, couldn't have been further from the truth. Instead, he put his $325 towards tiny lodgings in West Hollywood with a number of roommates, slept on a mattress on the floor, and set about making ends meet.

Brad's new-found bid for stardom wasn't entirely plain sailing at first, and like many young would-be thesps, he was forced to try and pay the rent by taking a number of dead end jobs. He started off by becoming a refrigerator delivery boy for local students, followed it up with a tele-sales job, trying to convince customers to buy tickets for a local police ball, and eventually became a limo driver for a strippergram company, chauffeuring the girls to their destinations, playing their choice of music, and then catching the clothes as they were flung left, right, and indeed, centre.

He soon swapped that for something a little bit more theatrical – donning a chicken suit and standing on the corner of Sunset and La Brea Boulevards in Los Angeles in order to entice passing folk into the nearby El Pollo Loco fast-food joint – and earned himself a not-to-be-sniffed at $9 an hour for his troubles. And while keeping himself out of financial straits, Brad attempted to eke out an acting career.

By this time he had set himself a goal – to become a successful actor within a year, or head home. But endless weeks of attending casting calls, meeting thousands of other young hopefuls and ultimately getting nowhere proved to be an almost soul-destroying process. With the exception of the chicken suit, the only thing he landed that was anywhere near an acting role was an extra's part in the Andrew McCarthy film *Less Than Zero.* Eagle-eyed viewers with a freeze-frame facility on their video recorders can in fact see Brad's screen debut, which consists of him merely standing in a doorway for all of two seconds. It may not exactly have been *Legends of the Fall,* but nonetheless he was on screen, and pocketed a very sizeable extras paycheque for his pains.

However, as the cycle of endless, fruitless auditions and string of odd jobs continued, Brad decided he needed to find an acting coach. When one of the strippers whom he escorted around in his limo offered to put him in touch with hers, he couldn't have been more delighted.

That coach was the late Roy London, a man who spurred the likes of Michelle Pfeiffer and Sharon Stone on to stardom. He taught Brad basics he had never even dreamed of, everything from delivering monologues to merely how to stand and breathe correctly on-screen. Despite the obvious complications of the process, Brad proved to be a fast learner. It was at this juncture that he landed himself an agent, after a woman in his class landed an audition with one, and persuaded Brad to take part in a scene she would be reading.

Naturally, Brad went along just to add moral support, but much to his amazement the agent ended up snapping him up instead of the would-be actress, noticing immediately that he had the sort of charisma and good looks that no amount of acting classes could ever produce.

Just one month later the TV roles began to dribble in. Significantly, these included a non-speaking role in the cult TV smash *thirtysomething* which, despite not even allowing Brad to say more than a single word on-screen was enough to bring him to the attention of *thirtysomething* producer and film director Edward Zwick, who years later cast Brad in the lead of the sprawling settlers saga that became the box office smash *Legends of the Fall.* There was also the popular daytime soap *Another World,* which signified Brad's first ever visit to New York City, an experience he found more invigorating than his short-lived part on the soap.

From Brad's point of view, though, perhaps the TV appearance that thrust him into the limelight was in the seminal 70s and 80s soap *Dallas.* Starring as the boyfriend of

Films, Fame and Fast Food

Top and *above:* Two examples of Brad's early days as a television star

Charlie, the wayward teenage daughter of Jenna Wade (Priscilla Presley), Brad found himself cast in the programme after going to an audition for the Sunday night series *Our House,* a short-lived show which starred the likes of *Beverly Hills 90210*'s Shannen Doherty. Failing to land the role, Brad was swiftly shipped next door where the producers of *Dallas* were in the middle of a similar casting call. And although the role lasted only a few episodes, as far as Brad was concerned, this was his big break, and finally the time to confess the truth to his parents, only to discover that they had guessed what he had been up to all along.

Although Brad's character, Randy, did not survive long enough to make much of a mark of *Dallas,* it was enough to turn Brad into something of a heart-throb, with requests for interviews at a premium, and teen magazines queueing up to feature him. He also got his first taste of intrusion on his personal life, with great interest placed on his relationship with *Dallas* co-star Shalane MacCall, who played Charlie Wade. Despite the eight year age gap, the pair were constantly in each other's company for two months, and were the centre of attention as far as the Hollywood media were concerned. However, Brad was too tied up with his career to become involved in a relationship, and the two went their separate ways once he was finished with *Dallas.*

Next up was a guest role in the smash hit sitcom *Growing Pains,* whose star, Kirk Cameron, was one of America's hottest heart-throbs at the time. The clean-cut 23-year-old had a chance to play against type, as a rugged transfer student who almost steals the heart of leading character Carol Seaver (Tracey Gold). Another guest role followed, this time in *21 Jump Street,* the cop show that made a star of Johnny Depp.

His next role, in the sitcom *Head of the Class,* not only lasted a few weeks longer, but was long enough for Brad to meet his next showbiz girlfriend, actress Robin Givens. Having recently broken up with husband Mike Tyson, she and Brad were together for six months.

But the TV roles were not enough for Brad. Against the advice of his agent, who was attempting to make him a major TV star,

he wanted to do a movie, and in 1989, that chance came his way. The film in question was *Cutting Class,* a low-budget, not exactly good, slasher movie that distinguished itself by being a spoof of such teen horror pics as *Nightmare on Elm Street* and *Friday The 13th.* Brad admitted it was a dreadful piece of work, but nonetheless, it was a significant step up the career ladder that not only put his face on the cinema screen for more than a few seconds, but also united him with his next actress girlfriend, co-star Jill Schoelen, whom he dated for two months before work split them up.

His second cinematic effort, *Happy Together,* starring Helen Slater and Patrick Dempsey, was forgotten equally quickly, although by this point he was landing leading roles in TV movies, including *The Image,* playing alongside Albert Finney, and an episode of *Tales From The Crypt,* in which he played a bike-fixated James Dean type who – naturally – met a sticky end.

But the film that was ultimately to change Brad's life was the 1989 TV movie *Too Young to Die.* Based on fact, it was a controversial piece focussing on teenager criminals receiving the death penalty, and starred Brad as the drug-addicted Billy, who was ultimately stabbed to death by his tormented lover Amanda Sue Bradley after he forced her to take drugs, and to earn money for him by becoming a prostitute.

As well as receiving much critical claim for a performance which cast him against type and required him to shed his pretty-boy image for that of a car-dwelling down-and-out (providing the first noticeable proof that he was capable of accomplishing more than just heart-throb status), the film also introduced Brad to Juliette Lewis, the actress who, despite being ten years his junior, was to become his first long-term actress girlfriend. Although the chemistry between the two was noticeable even while they played out harrowing scenes of drug addiction on-screen together, it wasn't until filming finished that they actually became an item in real life.

Brad's next career move proved less successful, taking on one of the four leads in a new prime time drama series, *Glory Days,* for the highly successful Fox Network.

Films, Fame and Fast Food

Top: The grungy anti-hero image of *Kalifornia*

Above: October 1992; Brad hangs out with then girlfriend Juliette Lewis

▶▶

Films, Fame and Fast Food

The cast of *Glory Days*: Stephan Alexander, Evan Mirand, Nicholas Kallsen and Brad Pitt

Having struck gold with *Beverly Hills 90210*, the producers felt that any project featuring a young, hip, not-exactly ugly band of leading actors would bring the viewers in. In the case of *Glory Days,* which focussed on the after-school lives of four best friends – including Brad as would-be newspaper writer Walker Lovejoy – and made its debut on July 25, 1990, they were wrong. The series lasted long enough to show the six episodes that had been filmed, before making a sharp exit from screens the following

September – despite being marketed as something new for the summer, a TV season traditionally filled with repeats.

Not that it made much difference to either Brad, who later described the deceased show as 'absolutely terrible," or to his career, as almost immediately, he was cast in another low-budget film, *Across the Tracks,* alongside former child star Ricky Schroeder. Although the film was overlooked at the box office, Brad's performance as Joe, a would-be athletics champion held back by his dropout elder brother Billy (Schroeder), gave him the chance to carry a movie from start to finish for the first time, as well as receiving much critical acclaim. Many reviews cited him as a star to watch.

By this time, he had been in Hollywood for four years and his career was rapidly gathering momentum. And those fans who were not content with his sporadic TV appearances could by now have their fill of Brad during commercial breaks, thanks to his new-found standing as the leading man in a long-running Levi's commercial. Having been released from some kind of tropical jail, Brad got to smooch with the leading lady, spin off into the sunset in a fast car, and even parade around in his undies, all to a backdrop of T-Rex's '20th Century Boy'. Although the advert was fundamentally for the European market, Brad had the kind of all-American good looks that were deemed necessary to provide Levi's with the proper promotion.

Despite all of Brad's initial success, however, the all-important major blockbuster still evaded him. While he and Juliette were still hopelessly in love, having moved into a rented bungalow in the suburb of Beechwood Canyon, and even talked of marriage, it suddenly appeared that work was about to separate the pair when she went off to play her breakthrough role in director Martin Scorsese's *Cape Fear*, a part that would eventually land her a Best Supporting Actress nomination at the Oscars. Brad, meanwhile, auditioned for a small but pivotal role in a movie which was set to star Geena Davis and Susan Sarandon, after the previously cast William Baldwin pulled out due to landing the lead in *Backdraft*. Without hesitation, he was cast in what eventually became *Thelma & Louise*.

Brad at London's Dorchester Hotel, while promoting *Legends of the Fall*

3

AN OVERNIGHT SUCCESS

Brad wins over cinema audiences everywhere as J.D. in *Thelma & Louise*

An Overnight Success

Top: Susan Sarandon and Geena Davis give Brad a lift in *Thelma & Louise*

Above: Geena, Brad and the "$6,000 orgasm"

Out of 400 hopefuls, Brad was cast as J.D. in Ridley Scott's *Thelma & Louise,* having had been noticed and recommended to the director by casting director Lou DiGiamo. Two auditions and three days later, he was on the set in Utah, unaware of the impact his few scenes would have on both the film's notoriety and his career.

The subject matter had already caused no end of controversy. Escaping from their no-good partners on what they believed to be a liberating fishing weekend, Thelma (Geena Davis) and Louise (Susan Sarandon), found themselves on the run from the law after one of them murders a would-be rapist. While trying to escape from the ever-closer

▶▶

clutches of the FBI, the pair pick up J.D, the hitch-hiker/con-artist who memorably gives Geena Davis' put-upon housewife her first orgasm, only to escape with $6,600 belonging to the beleaguered twosome, and forcing them to rob their way to the Mexican border, gradually getting into deeper and deeper trouble. The finale, which gives the women the option to either surrender and face jail, or drive headlong into the Grand Canyon (they sensibly opt for the latter), has ironic parallels with *Butch Cassidy and the Sundance Kid,* the first film Brad saw.

While Brad only occupied around ten minutes of screen time, those 600 seconds captured much attention and won him female admirers across the land. One of those most impressed was the then 15-year-old Gwyneth Paltrow who, on catching her first glimpse of Brad's prowess, watched the film completely unaware that the star she was seeing onscreen would not only one day be acting alongside her (in *Seven*), but would also be her partner in real life.

However, his impressive performance as the aforementioned dastardly charmer was unjustifiably overshadowed by the fact that he was required to dispense with certain items of clothing during what became known throughout the movie world as 'the $6,000 orgasm.' Although it fails to show through onscreen, Brad's biggest concern was not his sudden transition to big-time movie-making, but the filming of his much talked-about love scene with Geena Davis, and his anxiety that his mother would not approve of his antics with the six-foot star.

Naturally, the nature of the scene combined with Brad's habit of being seen on the arms of his co-stars set the Hollywood gossip mill in motion, with rumours that Brad had become Geena Davis' latest beau. Considering that Geena had just broken up with her husband, actor Jeff Goldblum, such a pairing provided perfect fuel for gossip columns countrywide – until, that is, all the rumours of Brad breaking his co-star's heart proved to be untrue. The pair had

Above: Looking very different in *The Favor*

Opposite top: The role that started it all; Brad as J.D. the con-artist in *Thelma & Louise*

never even been seen together anywhere except onscreen.

Fortunately, the film managed to overshadow the gossip mongers, opening in May 1991 to critical raves, Brad taking his share of the praise in many reviews and quashing talk of his involvement with Geena by turning up to the premiere with Juliette Lewis in tow. The film went on to break the $100 million mark worldwide at the box office, and failed to go unnoticed when Oscar time rolled around. Both Geena Davis and Susan Sarandon were nominated for Best Actress, and Ridley Scott was shortlisted for Best Director, although eventually the film's only gong went to the mantelpiece of its screenwriter, Callie Khouri. Not that Brad was too disenchanted. 'After the stuff I had done, it was a relief to be in something that important,' he said at the time.

Despite being offered no end of similar pretty boy roles as a result of this, Brad decided that diversity was the best career option – a move which, initially, turned out to be a mistake. Firstly, there was a supporting role in *The Favor* as Elliott Fowler, an artist in

In a scene from the quirky, off beat drama *Johnny Suede,* be-quiffed
Brad shares a tub and more with his co-star Tina Louise

love with a wealthy gallery owner (Elizabeth McGovern). Meanwhile, her best friend (Harley Jane Kozak), trapped into a life of housewifery and motherhood, is still fantasising about her high school boyfriend, only to chicken out when the opportunity of them spending the night together actually comes up. While McGovern steps into the fray to take her place, she soon discovers she is pregnant, and unable to tell whether the father is her one-night stand, or Elliot, with whom she was conducting an on-off relationship.

The film did very little at the outstet, as Orion, the company who made it, went into liquidation shortly after it was completed, leaving a back catalogue of films which went unreleased until a few years later. When *The Favor* eventually did surface in 1994, it was to lame box office and limp reviews – even Brad's standing as a superstar by that point had little effect. It eventually went straight to video outside the U.S.

However, Brad's next appearance at the pictures saw him styling his hair into a mammoth quiff and starring in the quirky *Johnny Suede,* the feature debut from cinematographer-turned-director Tom DiCillo. With a budget of just $500,000, it was a world away from *Thelma & Louise,* and starred Brad living in a dingy flat and a daydream world, wandering around in alarming underwear and harbouring a desire to be a rock star like his idol Ricky Nelson, after being hit on the head one day by a pair of black suede shoes tumbling from the sky. On the one hand, it gave him a chance to exercise his vocal cords for a cinema audience. On the other, Brad spent two hours every day having his hair fashioned into the quiff he sports in the picture, an experience he later described as 'close to torture.'

Released in 1991 complete with simultaneous premieres in both New York and Los Angeles, *Johnny Suede* captured more than its fair share of good reviews and won the Golden Leopard at the prestigious Locarno Film Festival in Switzerland, but failed to make a *Thelma & Louise*-esque impact at the box office. Meanwhile, the film's director Tom DiCillo went on to make the highly-acclaimed cult hit *Living In Oblivion,* a low-budget film about the perils of making a

An Overnight Success

low-budget film, whose release sparked a barrage of unfounded rumours that lead character Chad Palomino, a blond blow-waved narcissistic actor played by James LeGros, was in fact derived from DiCillo's experiences of working with Brad.

His follow-up film project, *Cool World*, seemed to have an aura of must-see about it at the time, and indeed, competition for roles was fierce. It promised to place Brad in an entirely animated world, but turned out to be just too brash and confusing for comfort.

Brad took on the role as a change of pace after having wowed director Ralph Bakshi, whose 1970s cult effort *Fritz The Cat* proved that cartoons were not always child's fare. He starred as Detective Frank Harris, a young soldier returning from World War II who, subsequently witnessing the death of his mother and believing himself to be responsible, is rescued by the cartoon-based Cool World, where he sets up shop as a detective. However, years later he is called upon to go back and save the real world when wayward animated femme fatale Holli Would (Kim Basinger) success-fully seduces cartoonist Jack Deebs (Gabriel Byrne), in an effort to become human, a move which would have disastrous conse-quences for all concerned.

Brad was as watchable as ever, but this did little to save the picture. Released in 1992, it captured abysmal reviews and died a swift death at the box office, to the extent that it was quietly trotted out elsewhere with the minimum of fuss.

While *Johnny Suede* may have been subjected to only a limited release and *Cool World* disappeared altogether, mainstream cinemagoers who had dis-covered the actor via *Thelma & Louise* were still able to get their fill of Brad. It was obvious that the failure of *Cool World* had failed to herald a death knell for Brad's career. By the time the film made its inauspicious debut he was already ensconced in Montana, mak-ing the movie that would ultimately enable him to be taken seriously as an actor as well as a teen heart-throb. The director in question was Robert Redford, the movie *A River Runs Through It*.

Above: Cartoon characters get frisky in *Cool World*

Left: *Cool World* sees Brad in private detective mode

Opposite: Brad and that hairdo in the off beat low-budget *Johnny Suede*

31

4

FISHING FOR COMPLIMENTS

Brad makes a splash in
A River Runs Through It

Initially, fly-fishing did not exactly sound like a sexy, scintillating topic for a major Hollywood movie, let alone a major Hollywood movie starring Brad Pitt. But when legendary sex symbol-turned-director Robert Redford began seeking his third directorial effort behind the camera, and decided Brad was the man he had in mind for the job of wandering around Montana rivers in thigh-length waders, the subject took on a whole new dimension.

Based on the autobiographical novella by Norman Maclean, *A River Runs Through It* is the author's story of growing up in a strictly religious family in 1900s Montana, where, according to the script, 'the only things a man is never late for are church, work and fishing.' As children, Norman (played by Craig Sheffer) lived in the shadow of his younger brother Paul (played by Brad); as adults, college and work separated them, and while Norman became a hard-working, upstanding family member, Paul opted for a job on a local newspaper and quickly slid into a downward spiral of drinking, gambling and flitting from one woman to another. While Norman was settling down with girlfriend Jessie (Emily Lloyd), Paul was out getting into brawls, getting thrown in prison, and getting into the sort of debts that even his job was unable to cover. But throughout it all, one thing remained constant: his love of fly-fishing, and his undisputed skill for splashing about in the river. A gentle, slow-moving and utterly absorbing piece of movie-making, it becomes obvious pretty early on that the denouement could only be a tragic one.

Although *Thelma & Louise* had made its own kind of impact, *A River Runs Through It* marked another turnaround in Brad's career, as landing the role of Paul gave him his first opportunity to carry a major motion picture on his own. Despite having taken the lead in both *Across The Tracks* and *Johnny Suede*, neither had made significant impact at the box office. Redford, whose own Sundance Film Festival (an event focusing on independently made movies) had shown *Johnny Suede* the previous year, had also considered the likes of Kiefer Sutherland and Robert Downey Jr. for the part. However, it took just one meeting with Brad to convince him that he was the man for the job.

The role required a great deal of preparation on Brad's part, with the basics of fly-fishing having to be learnt from scratch. For weeks beforehand he spent hours standing on rooftops in Hollywood – the only place where he could find enough room to cast his rod – practising the techniques, but despite landing the hook in the back of his head on a number of occasions (even once embedding the hook so deep that it had to be dug out with a pair of pliers) he quickly became quite proficient. Further fishing lessons in Montana, as well as mastering the local accent, were required before a single camera could roll on the project. In addition, his hair was dyed even blonder than usual to emphasise his standing as the dark-haired family's golden boy.

Working on the film proved to be a happy, laid-back experience for the new-found leading man. As well as spending a lot of quality time alone, soaking up the

Brad finally nets the big one in a scene from
A River Runs Through It

Fishing for Compliments

Top and *opposite:* Brad as fly-fishing golden boy Paul Maclean in *A River Runs Through It*

Above: Brad finally gets to spend some time with Juliette Lewis

Montana landscapes or reading in his rented accommodation, Brad also befriended a number of the actors with whom he worked, in particular bit-part player Buck Simmons, who landed a one-line role in the film after passing through Montana on his college vacation and responding to an advert in the local paper.

The pair got on so well that once filming had finished, Buck decided that the acting bug had bitten good and proper, and ended up becoming Brad's flatmate in his West Hollywood apartment. Sadly, things did not quite go the way he planned, and has never been seen onscreen since.

Ultimately, the extra work and research on Brad's part proved to be worth all the effort. While *A River Runs Through It* was never intended to be a hugely commercial it was eventually released to sterling reviews, gaining enough word of mouth to spur it on to a respectable $43 million gross in the U.S. 'Redford's proved that you can elevate film with really good material,' was Brad's response.

While it only landed a single Oscar (for the breathtaking cinematography, and landscapes which cry out to be viewed on the big screen), Brad's superb performance was not overlooked by any stretch, with many comparing him to a young Robert Redford – ironically, something the director had himself done upon first meeting his new star. Obviously not every review was positive, but audiences lapped up the way he could make even the act of catching a huge fish seem to be an excuse for celebration. Like it or not, he slipped into the skin of Paul Maclean so effectively that his character's untimely death was all the more heartbreaking.

Despite all the adulation, though, Brad was far from happy with his work on the film, feeling that he had failed to deliver the powerful performance that was required of him. 'There could have been a little more underneath,' he commented, 'but there was no getting round it.'

Indeed, Brad may have thought this, but it did his career no harm whatsoever. As well as being elevated into the same bracket as such other young major league Hollywood talent as Keanu Reeves, Christian Slater and Johnny Depp, he found that his potential was finally being realised, and there was indeed more to his talents than the pretty face and washboard stomach of *Thelma & Louise* fame.

But Brad still stood out as different from the rest, shunning the limelight and the inevitable paparazzi attention, preferring instead to concentrate on his career, partly the reason why he had been largely ignored by the media since the phenomenon of

►►

Thelma & Louise. And far from taking the romantic hero or squeaky-clean characters route that his good looks might have dictated, Brad was not only more concerned with taking the most interesting roles possible, but also spending more time with Juliette, whose own career was also blossoming by this point. The pair barely managed more than a few days together at any one time.

It was Brad's agent who managed to kill two birds with one stone by coming up with a script which would not only allow the two of them to star together, but would also allow Brad a total change of direction – a role that actually required him to look far from his best. The parts in question were that of sociopathic serial murderer Early Grayce and his child-like girlfriend Adele Corners. The movie went by the name of *Kalifornia.*

▶▶

This kind of thing never happened in *The X-Files* – David Duchovney and Brad in a Mexican standoff

Cute and Crazy – Brad as you've never seen him before

By this time it was apparent to the public that Brad and Juliette were an item, with a relationship that quite transcended the ten year age gap. On the surface it seemed to be an unlikely pairing. He hailed from a small Missouri town, and had had a steady upbringing in a happy family home, with his only thespian contact coming in the form of supporting roles in school plays. She, on the

other hand, was born in San Fernando, Los Angeles, the daughter of an actor, Geoffrey Lewis, and despite a similarly healthy parental relationship, had herself been bitten by the acting bug at a very early age, cropping up on sitcoms like *The Wonder Years* by the age of twelve. By the time she turned fourteen, she had been to court to have herself legally emancipated from her

▶▶

Kalifornia Dreaming

enormous book collections. The finishing touch was pets; Brad investing in a trio of dogs, and Juliette becoming the proud owner of a cat she simply christened Me.

And now, as the pair were named Male and Female Star of Tomorrow at the prestigious Nato ShoWest Awards in Las Vegas, they prepared to star onscreen once again, only this time at the movies.

Kalifornia, directed by first-time helmer Dominic Sena, couldn't have been further removed from *A River Runs Through It.* Released in 1993, when controversy over violent movies had reached a new high with the likes of *Reservoir Dogs* and *Bad Lieutenant* hitting cinemas, the film centred around a nice yuppie couple, writer Brian Kessler (*The X-Files'* David Duchovny), and photographer Carrie Laughlin (Michelle Forbes). Deciding to go on a tour of famous American murder sites as research for a book Brian is working on culminating their tour by arriving in California; to help share the cost of the trip they advertise for two people to go with them.

Unfortunately for them, the lucky pair turn out to be Early (Brad) and his waitress girlfriend Adele (Juliette). Early, who is first seen attempting to cause a car pile-up by casually hurling a rock over a bridge, is pure white trash – on probation, living in a trailer park with Adele and with no job prospects. When he joins Brian and Carrie on their jaunt, it isn't without having first murdered and robbed the landlord hassling him for his overdue rent, and setting fire to his trailer. However, it isn't until a fatal punch-up in a Texas bar that Brian and Carrie realise exactly what they have let themselves in for, as their cross-country spree develops a body count courtesy of their psychotic hitch-hiker.

What proved to be most shocking about the film was not only the way that Early casually murdered and robbed his victims (including his own girlfriend), but also how his new-found companion adapts to the violent acts he teaches him. The film ends

Top: The relationship continues onscreen; Brad and Juliette in *Kalifornia*

Above: The unwashed hair look of *Kalifornia*

parents and be declared an adult, in order to overcome child labour laws which only allow minors to work a certain number of hours per week. Having won the battle, she moved to Hollywood and moved in with her best friend, Trish Merkens.

But even though their early lives were poles apart, they soon found they had a lot in common, not least their taste in selecting projects, and the fact that both were pathologically career-minded. In 1992 they moved into a house in the Hollywood Hills together and began furnishing it to their like-minded requirements, and were spotted spending many weekends buying furniture in antiques shops around the area. The pair even emphasised their love of reading by reserving one room in the house strictly for their

▶▶

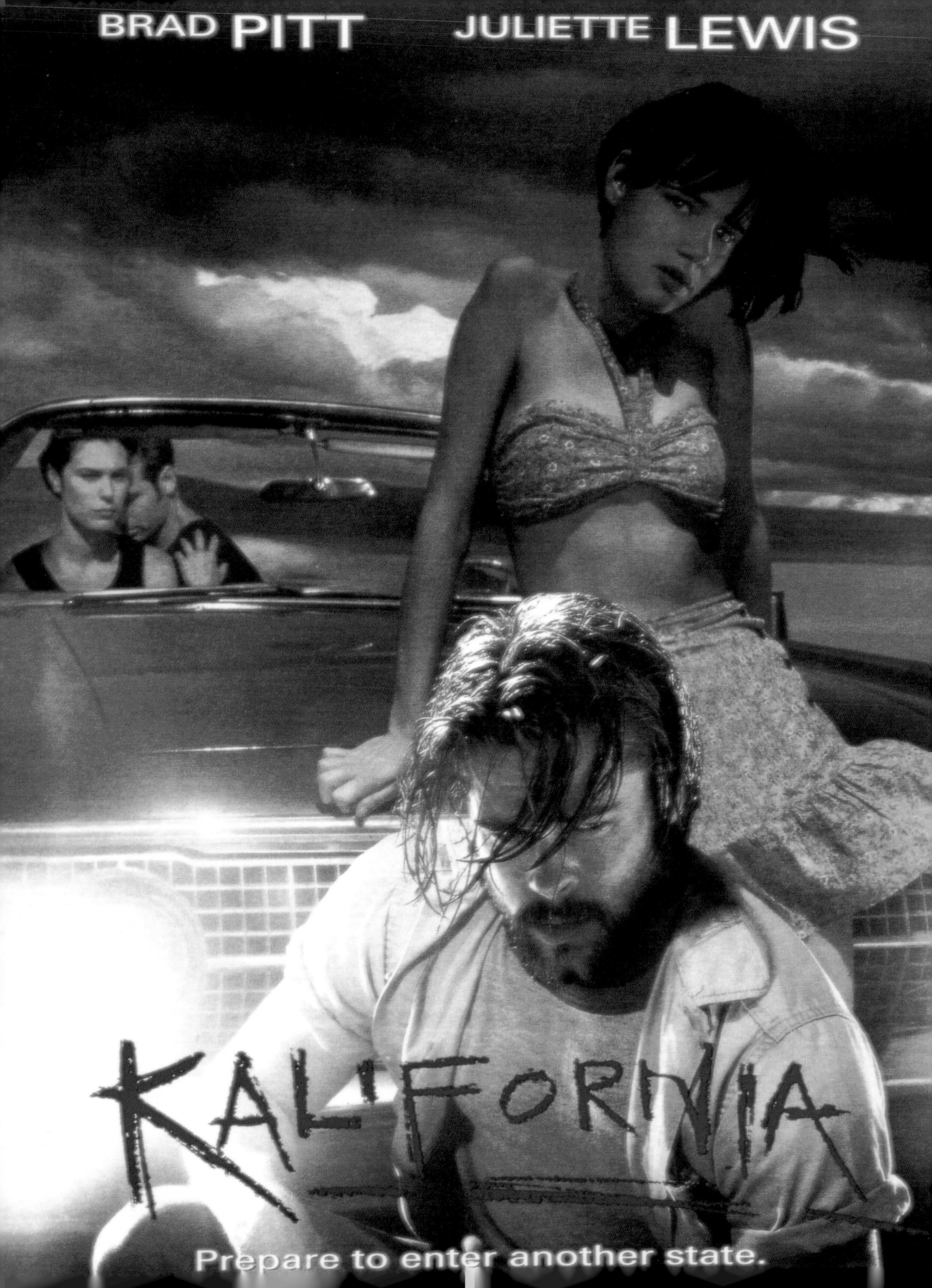
BRAD PITT
JULIETTE LEWIS
KALIFORNIA
Prepare to enter another state.

with Early taking the couple hostage, a finale that leaves only two of the quartet alive.

The change of pace required Brad to once again dispense with his heart-throb image. This he did to perfection, gaining 20 pounds in weight, growing a straggly beard and leaving his hair uncut and, for the most part, unwashed. 'It's the farthest thing from Golden Boy,' he said of his role in the movie.

With all its credentials, it's hard to ascertain why *Kalifornia* flopped so spectacularly at the U.S. box office. Brad and Juliette, by this point hot property in the film world, were both superb; him every inch the snarling, shambling, motiveless psychopath, her, reprising the little girl lost act that won her a Best Supporting Actress Oscar nomination in *Cape Fear.*

But when *Kalifornia* was released in the summer of 1993, the reviews were indifferent (although Brad's performance once again won him plaudits) and the public stayed away. It could have had something to do with the obvious competition from the blockbusters hitting screens at the tail end of a summer that included the likes of *Jurassic Park* and *Last Action Hero.* More likely to be the cause, though, was the fact that the movie was just too dark for mainstream consumption. While America is renowned for its fascination with serial killers (Juliette Lewis'

later turn as one such creature in Oliver Stone's *Natural Born Killers* achieved solid receipts), the character of Early had none of the glamour that attracted punters to the likes of Hannibal Lecter or even the mysterious John Doe whom Brad hunted down in his later box office smash *Seven.* Whether things would have been different if Brad had taken on the David Duchovny role remains to be seen.

'I needed the balance,' he explained later as to why he opted for bad guy duties. 'I don't believe in the all-your-eggs-in-one-bucket kind of theory. You get pushed in this business, you just gotta push back harder.'

Kalifornia may not have troubled the inside of cinemas as much as everybody hoped, but it didn't scupper Brad's bankability, even if he did find himself suddenly flooded with prospective serial killer roles. Once again, it was time for a change of pace, which the wunderkind director-screenwriter Quentin Tarantino ably provided.

The movie, *True Romance,* was also a flop Stateside, only this time mileage (and, indeed, cult status) was provided thanks to a screenplay penned by Quentin Tarantino and a release date just a few months after *Reservoir Dogs* had been unleashed on an unsuspecting world. Brad turned out to be just one of a number of stars queueing up to

Top: Brad as killer Early Grayce, clings to girlfriend Adele (Juliette Lewis)

Above: The Oscars 1992; Brad and Juliette happy together

▶▶

Kalifornia Dreaming

Stealing the show in director Tony Scott's
True Romance

apply their talents to whatever Tarantino had put to paper – the list included Christopher Walken as an evil hitman, Gary Oldman as a dreadlocked pimp who meets a sticky end, Dennis Hopper as the father of Christian Slater's gentle, comic-book loving hero Clarence Worley, and Val Kilmer as, of all things, the ghost of Elvis Presley.

In the film, Slater stars as a comic book shop worker who bumps into hooker Alabama Whitman (Patricia Arquette) while at the cinema on his birthday, and the pair, who seemingly have everything in common, fall in love, a situation which fails to change even after she tearfully confesses that she

was hired by Clarence's boss to make his birthday go with a bang. Undeterred, the pair marry the next day, only for Clarence to accidentally steal a suitcase full of drugs from his new wife's ex-pimp (Gary Oldman) and flee to Hollywood to pull off the deal of a lifetime and get away from the many hitmen on their tail. Brad provided the catalyst for the action to reach its explosive climax, by doing little more than lying on a sofa trying to remember exactly what had happened an hour previously – and practically stole the show. The character Floyd, the perpetually stoned flatmate of Slater's best friend, occupied less than ten minutes of screen time and took

only two days to film, but manages to unknowingly betray Clarence and Alabama to what seems to be every hitman in Hollywood.

Sporting a blond wig over his ever-increasing locks, Brad's portrayal proved he could make an audience laugh as well as act admirably.

'It was fun,' he said. 'But I was only there for a couple of days.' Taking on the role because it provided him with a chance to play somebody who creates general mayhem, Floyd was in fact based on an old friend of Brad's who came to stay for a week and ended up spending two years chez Pitt.

True Romance may have helped to cement Brad's status as a genuine all-rounder, but on the home front things were not so perfect. Soon after he completed his cameo role in February 1993, Brad and Juliette split, reportedly after he became commitment shy. She wanted to settle down and get married, he just wasn't ready to take such a serious step. Ultimately, it was

he who ended the relationship and moved out, leaving their dream home to her.

Naturally there was heartbreak on both sides – although the two were still in love, Brad felt it would be unfair to stay with somebody whom he was unable to commit himself to in such a way. Juliette sought solace in one of Brad's acting contemporaries, Johnny Depp, with whom she made 1993's underrated *What's Eating Gilbert Grape?* Brad, meanwhile, had a brief relationship with Jitka Pohlodek, an actress who had Czechoslovakian roots, but hailed from America's Deep South.

On the work front, Brad had taken it relatively easy since *True Romance*, getting over the break-up with Juliette and also waiting for another suitable project to come his way. The sabbatical came to an end at the end of that year when a duo of projects destined to catapult him to superstar status landed at his feet. One of these was *Interview With the Vampire*, the other *Legends of the Fall*.

Above: Jitka Pohlodek accompanies Brad to *Legends of the Fall*'s Los Angeles premiere

▶▶

6

THE GORY DETAILS

The Gory Details

A complete transformation for *Interview with the Vampire*

The gory goings-on in *Interview With the Vampire,* with Tom Cruise *(top),* Kirsten Dunst *(centre)* and Antonio Banderas *(above)*

Although *Legends of the Fall* was made before *Interview With the Vampire,* the latter was released first, giving Brad his biggest box office hit to date and officially sealing his status as a superstar.

With a cast to die for, including Tom Cruise, Christian Slater and the then lesser-known Antonio Banderas, it was a project that was destined never to be a failure. However, it nearly didn't happen at all. After years in the offing, bringing it to the screen proved to be a lengthy process after Anne Rice, the author of the novel on which the film was based, announced she was not only dissatisfied with the script, but was mightily peeved at the casting of Cruise as her beloved creation, the evil vampire Lestat. Previously Daniel Day-Lewis had been all set to take the role, and while director Neil Jordan and producer Stephen Woolley considered the likes of William Baldwin and Ralph Fiennes upon his departure they eventually came up with the idea of Cruise.

Brad, on the other hand, they had wanted for the role of the maudlin, suicidal bloodsucker Louis De Ponte Du Lac right from the beginning. The character in question is first seen in the present day, informing a reporter, Malloy (Slater) that he 'hasn't been human for 200 years,' and proceeds to tell the story of how he came to be in such a situation. Flitting back to the 18th century, Louis is a plantation owner in New Orleans who, seeking solace after the death of his wife and family, is persuaded into a life of neck-chomping, nocturnal activities, and eternal youth and immortality by the seductive, ruthless vampire Lestat (Cruise). While his conscience prevents him from murdering humans purely for their blood (cue lots of scenes of Brad biting the heads off rats and chickens to survive), he meets Claudia (Kirsten Dunst) who, having also fallen victim

to Lestat's charms, is similarly vengeful towards him for trapping her inside the body of a young girl – mentally she would be an adult, but her body would always remain child-like. Having apparently killed him, the pair flee to Paris, Lestat's birthplace, to try and discover more about his origins, but a spiral of events at the French capital's Theatre Des Vampires leads to a series of tragedies and an inevitably bloody conclusion. Having once again encountered the ageing Lestat in the present day, Louis feels it is time to share his story with said journalist. Meanwhile a neat final twist, perfectly suited to the film's dark overtones, paves the way for a sequel.

The film is one of Brad's best to date, a sweeping, majestic effort that captures the imagination as much as it unnerves (indeed, the copious blood-letting will not be to everybody's taste). The shoot, on the other hand, was not without its problems. Brad, having just come off *Legends of the Fall,* was exhausted, and admitted afterwards that filming had not been an entirely pleasant experience. 'My character is depressed from beginning to end; five and a half months of that is just too much,' he said. In addition, the first two days worth of filming had to be re-shot because the eerily pale make-up he was required to wear was too thick. Then on October 18, 1993, two weeks after filming began, River Phoenix, who had originally been cast as the reporter Malloy, died of a drugs overdose outside Johnny Depp's Los Angeles nightclub, The Viper Room. While Brad was shocked to hear of his co-star's death, a new kind of panic set in: the director needed to find a replacement. Christian Slater proved to be the ideal candidate, beating off competition from the heavily praised likes of Stephen Dorff and Leonardo Di Caprio.

Above: Claudia (Kirsten Dunst), Louis (Brad) and Lestat (Tom Cruise) search New Orleans for new victims

As well as shooting in New Orleans, Paris and San Francisco, much of the footage over five and a half months of principal photography was captured at Pinewood Studios, just outside London. During this time Brad took up temporary residence in London where, appropriately enough, considering the nature of the film on which he was working, he stayed at the old home of the late horror legend Peter Cushing. Far more to his disadvantage, though, were the long false black nails he was made to wear, which took so long to put on and remove that he contin-ued to sport them throughout the entire shoot, only removing them at weekends.

As the shoot drew to a close, rumours began to emerge that the project was troubled, not least because Brad and Tom had a strained relationship and that Tom had insisted on wearing platform-heeled boots during filming in order to see eye-to-eye with his co-star. Again, as with so much speculation, the whole thing turned out to be a myth. Admittedly, Tom had insisted on a closed set, made everybody involved with the film sign a form promising not to release any

▶▶

The Gory Details

spend their breaks working on what they termed their 'ugly wall', a space devoted entirely to Polaroids of each other pulling increasingly bizarre faces. Considering that Brad spent every working day playing a suicidal figure, those moments of light relief were enormously appreciated.

When Anne Rice finally saw the film, she was so impressed that she even went so far as to take a two-page advert in trade bible *Variety* expressing her utmost enthusiasm for the finished product and apologising profusely to Tom Cruise. It was this, together with an outburst from chat show queen Oprah Winfrey over the film's violent content, that helped boost the movie's opening weekend. While the presence of Tom Cruise and Brad Pitt was already a sure thing, the additional hype fuelled the movie on to take in a massive $38.7 million in its first three days on release, the fourth biggest opening of all time.

However, not all the reviews were good. Many attacked Brad's performance, suggesting that he was wooden and lacked screen presence, somehow forgetting that Louis was meant to have a kind of listlessness about him. It made no difference to the eventual gross: *Interview* went on to make over $100 million at the American box office alone. If there was ever any doubt that Brad Pitt had achieved megastar status, this silenced the critics and put paid to the theory once and for all.

Despite all the deserved adulation, he realised he needed to take a break, having done two such demanding roles back to back and feeling totally drained from the demands that playing Louis had made on him. His romance with Jitka Pohlodek (whom he had affectionately nicknamed Yit) came to an end shortly after he completed *Interview,* although they remain good friends to this day, and he was subsequently linked with the likes of Uma Thurman and rock star Courtney Love, both of whom inevitably again turned out to be just good friends.

Instead, Brad turned his attentions to

information about the shoot, and insisted that Brad and Kirsten be brought to the set through a specially constructed canvas tunnel so as not to see him in make-up.

But it made no difference to the relationships among the cast. Brad and Tom not only praised each other's performances to the hilt, they also spent some of their free time going go-kart racing together. Furthermore, their rapport with the then twelve-year-old Kirsten Dunst, who put in a remarkable performance as Claudia, was equally light-hearted. The trio would often

Top: **Louis De Ponte Du Lac on his estate**

Above: **Brad finally turns vampire hunter**

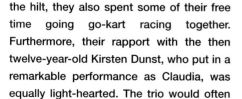

Above: The gothic home in Beachwood,
California that became Brad's home

investing in his very first property – an early
20th century dwelling that had once
belonged to US horror show icon Elvira and
came complete with a pool, pond and a
small cave, which Brad eventually deco-
rated with an ornate Oriental rug .

The house itself was ironically gothic,
bearing in mind the role that Brad had just
played. Complete with a green iron gate
bearing a design in the shape of a spider's
web, Brad relished the sheer detail that lay
within the walls of the three story dwelling,
including built-in glass cabinets and
detailed wood panelling. The huge grounds
not only provided room for Brad's menagerie
of pets to roam free , but also meant that the
house was hidden away, providing him with
some much-needed privacy.

Having moved in his collection of
antiques, his three dogs, Todd Potter, Saudi
and Purty, and forty pet chameleons that he

and Jitka had acquired. In fact, the actress's
penchant for unusual pets – she was the
owner of two bobcats when she and Brad
met – was believed to be one of the things
that attracted him to her, and indeed he went
on to keep the animals in his new home. To
put a lid on things, he spent some of his
earnings on six hundred acres of land in the
Ozarks, near his home town of Springfield, to
serve as a retreat when he wanted to get
away from it all.

Brad's next acting job was in *Seven,*
filmed at the start of 1995 just as *Interview
With the Vampire* was being released glob-
ally to similar hysteria, but just a few weeks
after its release he was back in the public
eye, this time attending the premiere of his
long-awaited previous project, *Legends of
the Fall*. If *Interview With the Vampire* had
made him hot property, this was the project
that was to extend that to boiling point.

▶▶

THE MAKING OF A LEGEND

The Making of a Legend

Country living comes easily to Brad

Legends of the Fall was a project that had been festering in the mind of director Edward Zwick since before his war epic *Glory* propelled Denzel Washington to Oscar stardom. Based on the novella by Jim Harrison, it chronicled three decades in the lives of the Ludlow family, Montana settlers who were torn apart by war, marriage and unlikely love triangles.

Brad played Tristan, the passionate middle son and focal point for much of what occurred. Kicking off with the move to Montana, Colonel Ludlow (Anthony Hopkins) finds himself abandoned by his wife who, unable to cope with her country surroundings, upped and returned to the big city, leaving him alone with their three sons: Tristan, Alfred (Aidan Quinn) and Samuel (*E.T.*'s Henry Thomas). Upon returning from college, the latter brings with him his fiancee Susannah (Julia Ormond), whom the other two are immediately smitten by, but the first tragedy strikes when Samuel enlists to fight in World War I, and is killed in action.

While Tristan believes himself to be responsible for his brother's death, he returned to the homestead and fell madly in love with Susannah, a situation which leaves him so guilt stricken that he leaves home for several years, returning to find that his older brother has married Susannah and his father has had a stroke that leaves him partially paralysed and unable to speak. He marries young native American Isabel Two, only for her to meet a tragic death at the hands of political opponents to his brother, who is by now a congressman in the nearby town.

Just when it looks as though things can't become any more tragic, Tristan wreaks murderous vengeance on his wife's killers while a grief-stricken Susannah commits suicide. Attempting to cover up the crime,

Top: The Tristan Ludlow facial hair phase for *Legends of the Fall*

Above: Looking far more clean cut with his screen father Anthony Hopkins

▶▶

The Making of a Legend

everything leads to a final showdown at the Ludlow ranch that almost decimates the family. Soppy and overly tragic it might be, this grand soap opera-esque saga is always

Top: **A tranquil moment for the Ludlow family**

Above: **Brad gets to grips with latest onscreen partner Julia Ormond**

watchable, with Brad's character Tristan sporting some uncanny parallels to Paul Maclean in *A River Runs Through It;* he is the only blond member of a unilaterally brunette family and in possession of a wild streak that bypasses his more conventional siblings and ultimately leads to his downfall.

Brad and the director had, of course, met previously when he was still a struggling actor trying to make a living, and had landed a one-word role on *thirtysomething.* For the first time, he had more of a hands-on involvement with a project; it was Brad, for example, who suggested that Aidan Quinn would be ideal to take on the role of Alfred, pointing out that they needed a person who 'would be an equal to Tristan.' Henry Thomas and Julia Ormond came on board soon after that.

Although the film is set in Montana, most of the shoot took place in the Canadian Rockies near the town of Calgary, where the Winter Olympics were held in 1988. It was a rushed affair: by this time Brad had already landed the part of Louis in *Interview With The Vampire,* and only had a certain amount

of time to complete Tristan duties before being whisked into the world of vampiric activity. To make matters easier, his scenes were filmed first, but despite the odd bout of friction between Brad and Ed Zwick, things went relatively smoothly.

But of course, the media bandwagon continued to roll. The topic of choice this time was the fact that for the duration of the shoot Brad had chosen to rent a nearby cottage and share it with his co-star, Julia Ormond. Naturally, it was immediately assumed that the pair were romantically entwined – but although Brad was prepared for the inevitable tabloid interest ('We knew that was coming, but it was completely about convenience,' he pointed out), he had little to fear as the living arrangement was purely a platonic one. As if further proof were needed, he spent many weekends hosting impromptu parties at his new hang-out, even inviting his brother, Doug, to spend a fortnight with him during the shoot.

Legends of the Fall made its debut to American audiences on Christmas Day, 1994, preceded by a premiere at which Brad showed his continued closeness to his family by flying them all out to Los Angeles to see the film – including his then heavily pregnant sister Julie. The film did not go on general release until January, the early opening on a single screen allowing it to qualify for the 1995 Oscars. Reviews were not entirely complimentary, and even Brad later admitted that the finished product turned out to be more of a slushy cinematic soap opera than he had first thought. Meanwhile, the Oscar-friendly marketing ploy failed to have the desired effect; although Brad's performance was recognised with a Best Actor In A Drama nomination at the Golden Globe Awards (he later lost out to Tom Hanks for *Forrest Gump*), the film managed to capture only one trophy come Academy Awards night – that of Best Cinematography.

While the Academy may have shunned *Legends of the Fall,* the film had an opposing effect on the public, with grosses nudging the $70 million mark in the States and, in the face of some lukewarm reviews, putting up a similarly good show elsewhere. If *Interview With the Vampire* had propelled Brad to superstar status, the swift release of

▶▶

Legends of the Fall made him something of a household name, with magazines, posters and adverts everywhere, and women of all ages falling for the tumbling blond locks and spirited, passionately romantic personality that he sported in the film.

He was ubiquitous, grabbing the covers of such prestigious magazines as *Vanity Fair,* and being voted The Sexiest Man Alive in the annual list compiled by top American publication *People.* Admiration came from the unlikeliest sources, including openly lesbian rock star Melissa Etheridge, who declared that Brad was the kind of man who 'could change a woman's mind.' The most bizarre story of the time sprang from that remark, suggesting that Brad had in fact taken on the job of sperm donor to the singer to enable her to have a baby with her lover. No prizes for guessing the amount of truth attached to this particular gem!

As with the cycles that had afflicted him following *Thelma & Louise* and *Kalifornia,* Brad immediately found himself on the receiving end of a number of intense but ultimately rather depressing films. Having finished *Interview With the Vampire,* he was offered lead duties in *A Simple Plan,* based on the novel by Scott Smith about a small-town accountant who finds over $4 million in an abandoned plane together with a dead pilot, and makes the decision to split the money between his brother and the latter's best friend, leading to deception, mayhem and mass murder. Tempting as it was, Brad turned it down; it was just too much. Another role that came Brad's way and veered in another direction was as New York's deputy mayor investigating corruption within his office in the Al Pacino-starrer *City Hall (*the part eventually went to John Cusack.

In the end, though, he opted to cut his hair and take on something which, while far removed from the romantic hero niche he had carved for himself with *Legends of the Fall,* required a cropped haircut, some murders guaranteed to have a lunch-losing effect on the audience, and material even bleaker than he had been required to tackle on his previous two projects. Not even Brad, however, could possibly have been prepared for the phenomenon that became the film *Seven.*

8

SAFETY IN NUMBERS

Brad, Gwyneth Paltrow and Morgan Freeman in a rare, non-horrifying moment from *Seven*

On the surface, *Seven* looked like another untypical Brad Pitt project. Directed by David Fincher, the man responsible for the film *Alien³* as well as putting his helming abilities to a number of pop videos (most notably Madonna's 'Vogue' and 'Express Yourself,' and the Aerosmith hit 'Janie's Got A Gun'), and penned by former Tower Records employee Andrew Kevin Walker as a reaction to his dislike of living in New York,

it focussed on a young rookie detective, David Mills, packed off to an unnamed town in America where he is partnered with the world-weary William Somerset (Morgan Freeman), a cop on the fringes of retirement. Mills has a young wife, his childhood sweet-heart Tracy (Gwyneth Paltrow), and in the film's only moment of light relief, they live in a dingy flat underneath a railway line with a constant flow of wall-shaking traffic.

▶▶

Safety in Numbers

seven

Detective Brad and the Seven Deadly Sins

Covering a seven-day period, the film follows Mills and Somerset as they attempt to track down a killer calling himself John Doe and knocking people off according to the Seven Deadly Sins – an obscenely overweight man, for example, is force-fed pasta until he dies from internal stomach haemorrhaging (Gluttony), a ruthless lawyer is forced to cut off a pound of his own flesh until he bleeds to death (Greed), a prostitute

is stabbed with a viciously adapted sex toy (Lust), and so on, and so on. Having led the cops halfway across the city, Doe eventually gives himself up two murders away from completing the septuplet – but naturally, things are not nearly as straightforward as they seem. The whole thing culminates in one of the most shocking, bleak endings to a mainstream Hollywood film in years.

However, Brad was insistent on following up *Legends of the Fall* in this way. At the time it seemed to be an unlikely premise, one that might just damage the pretty boy reputation that the likes of *Interview With the Vampire* and *Legends of the Fall* had recently landed the star. David Mills, the character in question, was a grungy, unattractive, possibly unhinged, being, a scenario that boded ill considering that it was the movies featuring a well-groomed, clean-cut Brad, that had to date raked in the most money.

▶▶

'The guy has no problems. That's the key thing'

Fincher soon changed his mind after a lunch meeting with Brad, in which he outlined that *Seven* was to be no run-of-the-mill blockbuster. Despite this, Brad displayed an unexpected enthusiasm for playing the part, literally begging the director to cast him.

Once on board, he proved to be instrumental in retaining the original, horrific ending, snubbing the kinder, gentler, more commercial finale that New Line Cinema chief Arnold Kopelson had suggested, and refusing to make the movie any other way. Oddly Brad took on the role because it appeared to be less emotionally draining or depressing than his previous two films. 'The guy has no problems. That's the key thing,' he cited as his reason.

Enthusiasm aside, the route to getting *Seven* on the screen was littered with both memorable occurrences and major pitfalls. For starters, Los Angeles was going through a particularly rainy season while the cameras were rolling, yet filming could not be delayed until the sun came out, owing to Brad's tight schedule which gave him just 55 days to get *Seven* into the can before moving on to his next project, playing alongside Bruce Willis in the Terry Gilliam-directed *Twelve Monkeys.* The troublesome weather was eventually incorporated into the finished film to startlingly good effect.

More seriously, and as a result of opting to do many of his own stunts, Brad's prowess in this particular department nearly had tragic consequences. During one take, he succeeded in smashing his left arm through a car windscreen, requiring urgent hospital attention for the resultant nerve and tendon damage he sustained and losing all sensation in his arm at the same time. To this day, the damage is still not fully healed, but shrugging off the suggestion that his hand would be rendered useless for life, Brad

managed to complete the film by either hiding his hand in his pocket or wrapping it in his coat. While his biggest concern at the time was whether the scene in question, featuring Brad racing across car roofs on a busy street, had been captured by the cameramen, the actual footage failed to make it into the finished film.

Fortunately, it wasn't entirely bad news, as it was on the set of *Seven* that Brad met his wife to be – the waif-like Gwyneth Paltrow, who plays the small but vital role of his onscreen wife Tracy. Gwyneth is the daughter of actors Blythe Danner and Bruce Paltrow, and has starred in the likes of *Flesh and Bone* with Meg Ryan and Dennis Quaid, *Mrs. Parker and the Vicious Circle* with Jennifer Jason Leigh, the Merchant-Ivory production *Jefferson In Paris,* and, most recently, as one quarter of a female bonding ring in the yet-to-be-released *Moonlight and Valentino.* The 22-year-old actress first caught sight of the man who was to become her fiance when, aged 15, she saw him onscreen in *Thelma & Louise.* The two are so devoted that not only are they renowned for major displays of public affection, but when Gwyneth was recently filming the lead in the latest movie adaptation of Jane Austen's *Emma,* over in England (in the West Country), Brad popped over to Dorset so he could be with her. But it isn't the first time the couple have been distanced by miles – while Brad resides in Los Angeles, Gwyneth still prefers to call New York home.

Seven was released in the US on September 22, 1995, the same day as the much-hyped *Showgirls,* Paul Verhoeven's close-to-the-knuckle account of Las Vegas strippers that received the kiss of death NC-17 rating Stateside. However, come the following Monday morning, the evidence was there for all to see: David Fincher's

Several killings later, Brad's patience snaps

▶▶

Safety in Numbers

Top: Brad discovers what greed can do to you

Above centre: Brad as David Mills, Morgan Freeman as jaded detective William Somerset

Above: Brad and Morgan with *Seven's* producer Arnold Kopelson

comparatively low-budget, terrifying and bleak serial killer thriller had trounced its opponent, taking over $13 million to Showgirls' $8 million. Not only was the film's non-universal subject matter drawing the crowds, but this provided further proof, if any were needed, that Brad had established himself as a star name capable of opening a movie. By the end of 1995, *Seven* had not only enjoyed a four week run at the top of the

US Box Office chart, but had gone on to take in an unprecedented $91 million, making it the biggest hit of the autumn season in the United States.

But that wasn't all. On its UK release on January 5, 1996, *Seven* spearheaded a remarkable box office achievement, namely the biggest collective box office weekend ever in the UK. A record previously held by the opening weekend of *Jurassic Park,* three

films, *Seven, Babe,* and *Ace Ventura: When Nature Calls* all grossed over £1 million at the box office, with *Seven* in fact scoring itself a massive three day opening of £2.6 million – ironically the seventh biggest opening for a movie in the UK. Ironically, while the UK National Lottery had six months previously taken the rap for driving people away from the cinema, *Seven's* bonanza occurred on the weekend that the first double rollover jackpot occurred and National Lottery hysteria reached an all-time high. Two weeks later, the film topped the charts on the second biggest box office weekend of all time, as *Seven, Babe* and the Michelle Pfeiffer starrer *Dangerous Minds* all surpassed the million mark to sandwich themselves comfortably between the two other record-breakers, providing further proof of Brad Pitt's enormous selling power.

Above: Brad and Gwyneth try to be incognito in some nifty matching shades

Above left: A million cinemagoers dive for cover as Brad and Morgan uncover yet another deadly sin

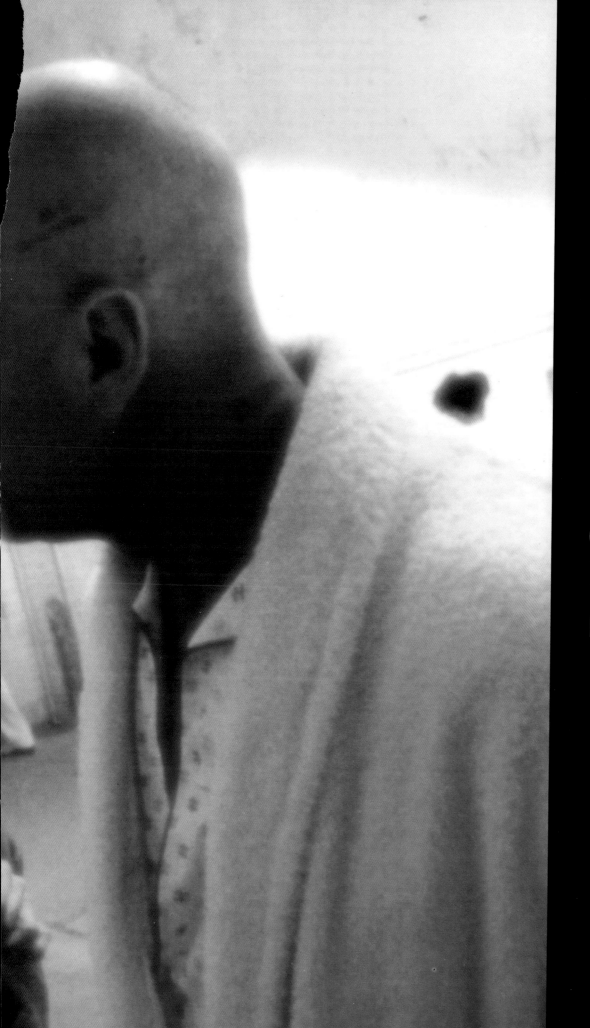

9

THE FUTURE

The Future

Oscar nominee for *Twelve Monkeys* – the future looks good for Brad

With his asking price rocketing from $3.5 million for *Interview With the Vampire* and *Legends of the Fall* to something approaching the $8 million mark, Brad has managed to cement his status as possibly the busiest star in Hollywood with four film projects.

First, in a move even further away from the chiselled handsome heroes he shot to prominence playing, there was the afore-mentioned *Twelve Monkeys* where, he has another crack at playing a bad guy. The movie stars Bruce Willis as a time-traveller sent back to the present day to prevent a deadly virus from wiping out half the world's population. Released in the United States on Christmas Day 1995, the film not only picked up plenty of favourable reviews and made it on to a number of critics' 20 Best of 1995 Lists, but also landed Brad his very first major award.

On January 21 Brad surpassed all expectations and picked up the Golden Globe for Best Supporting Actor. He beat hot favourite Kevin Spacey who had won every Supporting Actor accolade going for his work in *The Usual Suspects* and *Seven*, and had been nominated at the Globes for his performance in the former film. Although it is far from being a sure thing, these awards, given out just a few weeks before the Oscar nominations are announced, are seen as a pointer as to just who will be most likely to walk off with a coveted gold statuette come Academy Awards night.

In addition, *Twelve Monkeys* provided further proof of Brad's inimitable pulling power by amassing a $14 million opening weekend, and hitting the $45 million mark after a month, despite suggestions that Terry Gilliam's weird, off-beat vision would prove just too much for mainstream cinemagoers

to take. Sporting the exact same cropped haircut as in *Seven* at the start, before going on to re-sport the luxuriant blond tresses of *Interview With the Vampire* and *Legends of the Fall,* Brad once again gets the chance to display his dark side – this time as faintly psychotic mental patient Jeffrey Goines, who first meets Bruce Willis' futuristic time traveller when the two of them are incarcerated in the same hospital.

To fully prepare for the role, Brad spent several weeks at the psychiatric ward of the Temple University Hospital in Philadelphia, where the film was made – except he took the radical step of actually going there in character, facial ticks and all. It proved to be a vitally useful research project, as Jeffrey was based on many of the characteristics of the patients that he met there. Brad even took the step of partially shaving his head and developing a hypnotic stare, claiming that he played the character as a kind of Charles Manson figure. Either way, the role is yet another significant departure.

Also being primed for award status, and due to hit cinemas in the autumn of 1996 is *Sleepers,* which Brad spent much of winter 1995 filming in New York. Based on the best selling novel by Lorenzo Catterio, it tells the true story of a group of friends' experiences in New York's notorious Hell's Kitchen during the 1960s, their ill-treatment upon being sent to a reformatory, and the vengeance they exacted on the people who ruined their formative years. Brad joins an all-star cast that includes Robert De Niro, Kevin Bacon and up-and-coming British actress Minnie Driver (*Circle of Friends*).

Next up for Brad will be *Devil's Own,* giving him not only a second stab at villain duties but also the chance to act alongside

Top: In *Twelve Monkeys,* Brad introduces himself to time traveller Bruce Willis

Above: Brad squeals his way to an Oscar nomination

▶▶

Top and above: Brad on the set of Sleepers, filmed in New York

Right: Brad receives a Best Supporting Actor Golden Globe for his work in Twelve Monkeys

Harrison Ford. Currently filming, Devil's Own stars the latter as a retired cop who gives shelter to a young homeless man, only to discover that he may or may not be an IRA terrorist.

Beyond this particular project, Brad is looking likely for the lead in Seven Days In Tibet. Based on another true story, this will see Brad starring as German World War II pilot Heinrich Harrer, who escaped from a British prisoner of war camp in Nepal by fleeing over the Himalayas to Tibet and become friendly with religious guru the Dalai Lama.

Ahead of this, Brad is not entirely sure what his next move will be, although suggestions have ranged from a long-in-the-offing biopic of James Dean, right through to the life story of blues guitarist Stevie Ray Vaughan, who was killed in a helicopter crash. Talk is still rife of a sequel to Interview With the Vampire, called The Vampire Lestat. There also exists the possibility of a movie version of the novel All The Pretty Horses by Cormac McCarthy, a book which Brad was so fond of that he is the voice that

can be heard reading the audio version. And following the Golden Globe, there exists the possibility of Brad collecting his very first Oscar, having been nominated as Best Supporting Actor for Twelve Monkeys.

However, whatever he decides to do next, one thing remains certain: success has not changed him, and Brad will remain the down-to-earth country boy he was when he first arrived in Hollywood poor and hopeful the best part of a decade ago. For example, he still drives a battered old jeep, preferring to spend his earnings on antique furniture for his home rather than splash out on a smarter set of wheels. He remains close to his family, especially his nieces and nephews, and hopes to add to the Pitt brood over the next few years by having a family of his own.

On the 600 acres he bought outside Springfield he will be building a house so that he can spend more time near his family. And away from the screen, his interests are many and varied. He is fanatical about music, with his huge CD collection covering genres from rock and jazz to blues; indeed, he still harbours a desire to follow in the footsteps of contemporaries Keanu Reeves and Johnny Depp and become a rock star. He owns three guitars and is extremely fond of jamming sessions. Brad also enjoys hanging out at some of Los Angeles' swankier nightspots, in particular LunaPark where his long time acting friend, Dermot Mulroney, sometimes performs with his own band. However, he is content taking long walks on the beach or just spending time at home as he is clubbing. Then, of course, there is the perennial favourite of art and architecture. Brad still makes time to sketch and design furniture, a move which has proved so successful he's even thinking of opening a shop which sells just that.

In short, it's been a long, not entirely easy road to the top. But now, with his salary at an all time high, with his career having reached the stage where he is able to pick and choose his roles, with scripts streaming in, with the days of fruitless auditions long gone, and his picture on the front of magazines a piping hot selling point, it would seem that at this stage in his career he can just do whatever he likes.

▶▶

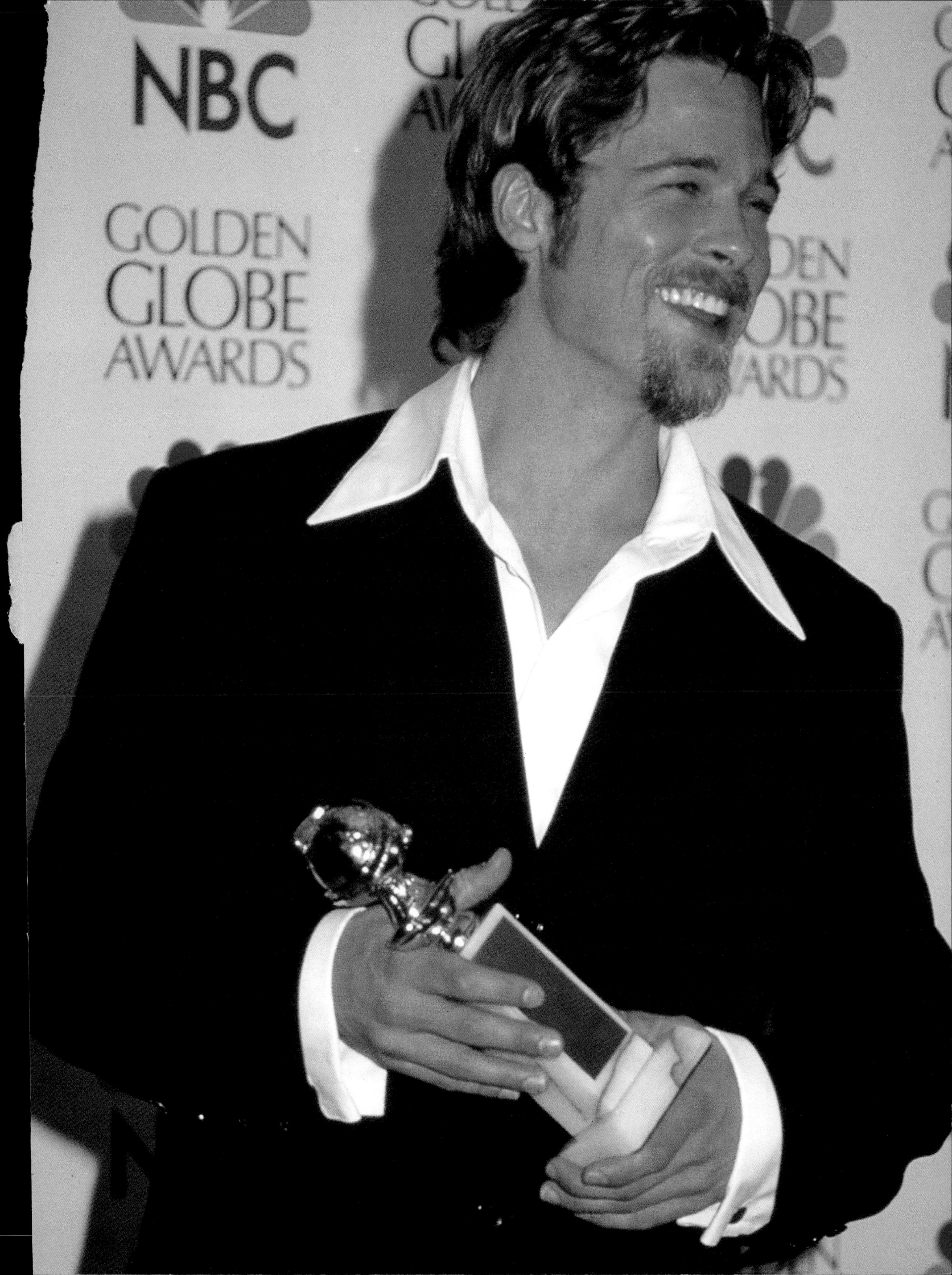
NBC
GOLDEN
GLOBE
AWARDS

REVIEWS

The following section contains an at-a-glance guide to the best and worst of Brad's career, featuring every cinema-released movie he has ever starred or appeared in . . .

Thelma & Louise

(1991) ★★★★★

Although Brad had little to do in this brilliantly crafted, eminently watchable female road movie, his was a pivotal role. Geena Davis and Susan Sarandon are the best friends who rebel against the men in their lives and take off together for a harmless fishing weekend, which quickly turns into a cross-country chase movie after one of them murders a would-be rapist. Brad, as the cowboy con-artist who masterminds Thelma (Davis') sexual re-awakening while the pair are on the run, appears initially to be all charm, but in a movie where the only sympathetic male character would appear to be Harvey Keitel's cop, is quickly re-located on to the ever-growing pile of bastards.

Johnny Suede

(1992) ★★★★

Brad's bizarrest role to date sees him donning a towering quiff to play the eponymous Johnny, a down-on-his-luck would-be rock and roll singer who spends most of his life wandering around his dingy flat in some equally dingy undies, until he suffers a knock on the head from a pair of blue suede shoes that tumble from the sky and things change dramatically. A quirky,

off-beat and amusing effort that served as the perfect antidote to Thelma & Louise's macho posturing, this is worth a watch if only to see Brad's excellent performance, alarming haircut, and musical prowess, with Johnny' s musical numbers being performed by the man himself.

Cool World

(1992) ★

It must have seemed such a good idea at the time – to have Brad Pitt as the only flesh-and blood character in a world populated entirely by cartoon characters. Unfortunately, Who Framed Roger Rabbit this is not. Brad is the snappy suit-wearing, be-quiffed private eye who escapes a personal tragedy by entering into the Cool World – a parallel universe where everything is animated, only to have to rescue the world he left behind when vampy toon Holli Would (Kim Basinger) mates with ace brush-wielder Jack (Gabriel Byrne) in order to become human. Sadly, an ingenious plot does little to detract from a weak script, lack of humour and cartoon characters that are more nightmare grotesque than Disney cute, while some cosmic mumbo-jumbo about worlds colliding only serves to complicate matters further. And Brad's ultimate

▶▶

conversion into cartoon form looks so unlike him as to be insulting.

A River Runs Through It
(1992) ★★★★

Fly-fishing may well be considered a trivial, boring, pursuit, but with Brad on board it turns into a thrilling, touching adventure. Directed by Robert Redford, it's the true story of two brothers, with Pitt as the younger, rebellious Paul, and Craig Sheffer as the sensible, down-to-earth sibling Norman, who are brought up under strict religious guidelines yet still somehow have time to become expert fly-fishers. Brad gives his best performance to date as Paul, the initially law-abiding golden boy who becomes a journalist and descends helplessly into a stream of alcohol and gambling addiction that inevitably leads to a series of tragic happenings. Through it all, though, he still manages to prove expert with a fishing rod. A very long, slow-moving film that spans years and feels like it lasts that long, but is so beautifully made and well-acted that the watcher almost begins to feel like a part of the family by the end.

The Favor
(1994) ★★

Released briefly in US cinemas, this little-known Brad vehicle sat on the shelf for two years, after the production company Orion, who made the film, went bankrupt. Having surfaced briefly at the flicks before being buried Stateside, it then oddly bypassed both the cinema and video rental markets in the UK before surfacing on video retail in 1994. Harley Jane Kozak stars as a happily married but bored woman who dreams of a night of passion with her high school ex, only to chicken out and persuade a single friend to bed the man in question instead. But here's the crunch – the hunky footy star isn't played by Brad! No! Brad just pops up in supporting role friend mode. Perhaps if he had taken the lead, things might have been very different. As it is, this uneasy, muddled romance is one for seriously devoted fans only.

True Romance
(1993) ★★★★

Another small but vital role for Brad, this violent Quentin Tarantino-scripted road movie has Christian Slater and Patricia Arquette as newly-weds on the run after accidentally stealing a stash of cocaine from Arquette' s pimp (Gary Oldman). Despite the violence quotient, this is a sharp, hilarious and compulsively watchable piece of work, decked out in vibrant colours and commanding near-perfect performances from all involved. Brad, meanwhile, is the hilariously drugged-out flatmate who doesn't even appear to know the time of day, yet almost manages to give the whole game away when the heavy mob finally turn up on his doorstep. His few small moments of perfection not only prove that he can do comedy as well as straight acting, but also leave you wishing that he appeared on screen for longer, being just one of many highlights in a film destined for classic status.

Kalifornia
(1993) ★★★★

Boldly cast against type, this has Brad starring with his then girlfriend Juliette Lewis as Early and Adele, a couple who hitch a ride with an upwardly mobile twosome on a tour of famous American murder sites. Naturally, the bearded Brad turns out to be a complete psycho and things go from bad to worse as murders (orchestrated by you-know-who) and mayhem pile up and the nice young pair who so kindly pulled over by the roadside in the first place are sucked into a down-ward spiral. Doomy and pessimistic, Brad ditches his trademark good looks for a spot of grunge, and comes across as a suprisingly convincing bad guy, although Lewis' little-girl-lost squeals begin to grate after a while. Cult buffs may like to note that the male half of the other couple is played by The X-Files' David Duchovny.

Interview With the Vampire
(1994) ★★★★

Poor old Brad gets it in the neck from Tom Cruise as the 18th century landowner who, seeking solace after the death of his

▶ ▶

wife, is initiated into the world of garlic-avoidance and neck-chomping by the demonic vampire Lestat (Cruise). Over 200 years down the line, having discovered that immortality and eternal youth are perhaps not such major assets he tells his story to reporter Christian Slater, ranging from feeding on rats and poodles to get his daily fix of the red stuff, to his revenge on Lestat together with an equally bitter 12-year-old vampire (Kirsten Dunst) doomed to stay a child forever because of her new-found status. Also starring Antonio Banderas, this is a lavish, awesomely mounted piece of work that stands streets ahead of other recent entries into the vampire genre. A must for Brad fans.

Legends of the Fall

(1994) ★★★

Featuring more tragedy than you can shake a stick at, this sprawling saga sees Brad as the spirited middle brother of three in a family of Montana settlers during World War I. Having been packed off to fight and failing to save his little brother (*E.T.*'s Henry Thomas) from death on the battle-field, Brad returns to the family fold, only to fall for the English fiancee (Julia Ormond) that his younger bro left behind. Trouble is, the eldest (Aidan Quinn) is similarly inclined, so beginning one of the most complicated movie love triangles in recent history. Tragedies are poured on one after the other (suicide, terminal illness, etc,

etc.), while Brad's character smoulders effectively, but is blessed with a bizarre tendency to run away and come back with a beard every time things don't quite turn out the way they should. An entertaining but rather daft elongated soap opera.

Seven

(1995) ★★★★

The sort of movie that requires either nerves of steel or stiff drinks to be given out with the purchase of tickets, *Seven* gives Brad his toughest role to date, as loose cannon cop David Mills who is teamed with wise old Morgan Freeman, a seen-it-all-before policeman nudging retirement. The task is to track down a killer who is murdering his victims in the manner of the seven deadly sins. A dark and doomy but brilliant piece of work, made even stronger by the total lack of murders onscreen – only the aftermath and graphic descriptions of the killings are given. Brad, meanwhile, manages to be shocked, tough and touching (in the relationship with his onscreen wife Tracy, played by real-life beau Gwyneth Paltrow) all at once, and is required to participate in one of the bleakest, most harrowing endings in a mainstream movie for a while.

Twelve Monkeys

(1995) ★★★★

A nightmarish vision of the future from Monty Python veteran Terry Gilliam, this

provides further proof that Brad is getting better with every part he turns his hand too. True, he only occupies about half an hour of screen time in this two and a quarter hour tale, but it's an electrifying performance that ought to secure him his first Oscar, if nothing else. Bruce Willis stars as a man from the future sent back to the present to track down the cause of a mysterious virus that wipes out 5 billion people during 1997, but he ends up trapped in the wrong time. Naturally nobody believes him and it isn't too long before he is swiftly dispatched to the loony bin, where he meets deranged animal rights activist Jeffrey Goines (Brad). Having eventually made it to 1996, he teams up with sceptical shrink Catherine (Madeleine Stowe), and sets off in search of an underground splinter group known as the Army of the Twelve Monkeys, whom he believes were responsible for the destruction – only no prizes for guessing who their leader is . . . Brad is a revelation here, all facial ticks and diatribes about the state of the nation one minute, ponytailed rich kid living in huge mansion with wealthy dad the next. It's strange, certainly, but this multi-layered thriller with more red herrings than you can shake a fish at is so well-crafted (even in the last half hour when it drops its previous plotlines and becomes a love story) and packed with clever moments you'll be hooked even when Brad isn't onscreen.

▶▶

Putting on a Play

THE CHIEF'S BRIDE

AN AFRICAN TALE

Written by Jenny Powell
Illustrated by Adrienne Kennaway

ABOUT THE PLAY

The Chief's Bride can be used during Shared or Guided Reading sessions with individuals or small groups of children. It can also be performed by the class with named parts given to individual children and the rest of the class playing the parts of the extra villagers, the washer-women and the trees.

This play is a valuable tool for use in the Year 4 Literacy unit 3 'Stories from other Cultures' or within unit 5 about 'Plays'.

Sets and props

Creating the sets and finding the props can be just as much fun as putting on the performance! You could tape together some white paper to make some backdrops that you then paint to create the sets; you would need a backdrop for a village house, the road that the daughters travel along, the forest and river and the Chief's house.

You can perform the play without having to find lots of different props. For example, furniture for the two houses could be your classroom tables and chairs. You will need some trees to represent a thick forest – these could be made from long wrapping paper tubes and strips of green crêpe paper. You will also need some clothes for washer-women to wash – think about the sort of clothes they would be washing, such as Zimbabwean prints and other African clothing. The food Daya gives on her journey could be some plastic food or just something wrapped in a cloth to represent food.

Staging

There is no need to put on a huge production. All you need is a large enough space for a stage and room for an audience. If you have access to an outside space and the weather is good, you can even put on the play in the open air! This would be a fantastic setting for the journey that Maiba and Daya make from their village to the Chief's village.

Costumes

You'll need to think about the traditional dress worn in Zimbabwe for your costumes. Traditionally, Zimbabwean women wear beautiful big beads and ornaments. The central part of the male clothing is the 'breastplate' (or Iporiyana), which is a large piece of animal skin worn around the neck. You could design and make your own Iporiyana. The animals Maiba and Daya meet on their journeys could be represented by puppets that you have made in class.

HAVE FUN PUTTING ON YOUR PLAY!

Go to www.waylandbooks.co.uk for more ideas.

Introduction

The play is based on the tale *The Story of Five Heads* by George McCall, told in his book *Kaffir Folk-lore*, published in 1886, and retells a Zimbabwean folktale. The tale was originally told by people living amongst the ruins of what was once the capital city of the Kingdom of Zimbabwe. Despite being a nineteenth-century folktale, the story's moral that kindness and goodness will always be rewarded still rings true today.

The characters in the play

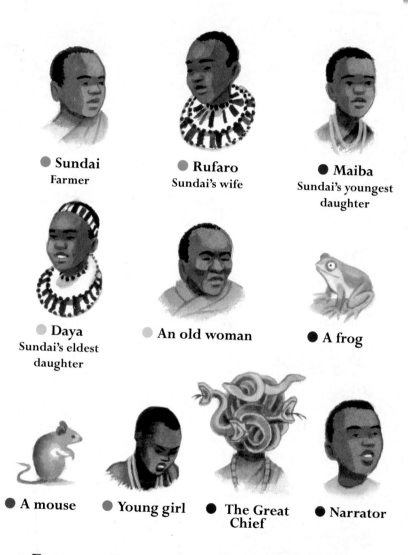

Sundai
Farmer

Rufaro
Sundai's wife

Maiba
Sundai's youngest
daughter

Daya
Sundai's eldest
daughter

An old woman

A frog

A mouse

Young girl

**The Great
Chief**

Narrator

Extras: *villagers, the bridal party, washer-women,
the wind and the trees.*

SCENE 1

CHARACTERS IN THIS SCENE:

- **Narrator** ● **Sundai** ● **Rufaro** ● **Maiba**
- **Daya** ● **Extras – Villagers**

Sundai is sitting down to eat breakfast as the sun rises in the village. Maiba and Daya enter the hut to greet their father. Villagers are listening in the doorway.

● **Sundai:** Good morning, Maiba. Good morning, Daya. I need to talk to you both about something very important.

● ● **Maiba and Daya:** Yes, Father. What is it?

● **Sundai:** Yesterday, I travelled to the village beyond the river. I spoke with the villagers there and they say that the Great Chief is looking for a wife. Your mother and I think one of you should go to the Great Chief.

● **Maiba:** (*forcefully*) Father, it **must** be me who goes to the Great Chief. I want to be admired and respected across the land. I will surely be so if I am the wife of a Great Chief.

● **Villagers:** (*whispering*) Maiba's a proud young girl. Maybe the Great Chief won't want such a proud wife?

● Narrator: Sundai and Rufaro do not want to listen to the gossip of the villagers. They love their daughter and agree Maiba should go to the Great Chief.

Rufaro: (*excitedly*) You should go soon, Maiba. No time must be lost!

Sundai: (*nodding*) Indeed, you shall go tomorrow.

Maiba smiles smugly to herself.

Narrator: Maiba knows that as the wife of the Great Chief she will be rich beyond her wildest dreams.

Sundai: I will gather a large bridal party to escort you. The Great Chief will be most impressed.

Maiba: (*angrily*) No, Father, I do not want anyone to come with me. I will go alone.

Daya: (*gasps and covers her mouth with her hand*) How can you say such a thing, Maiba? You know that you must have a bridal party. It is the custom in our village.

Rufaro: I agree. Don't be foolish, Maiba, you must have a bridal party!

Maiba: (*proudly*) I am not foolish, Mother, and I will have my way. I shall go alone.

● A villager: (*whispering to the other **villagers***) What is Maiba thinking? Surely the Chief won't accept her as his wife without a bridal party?

● Narrator: Sundai knows his daughter is strong-minded and will not be persuaded.

*Pause whilst **Sundai** thinks about what to do. At last he speaks.*

● Sundai: (*nodding at his daughter*) Very well, my daughter, you may do as you wish.

SCENE 2

CHARACTERS IN THIS SCENE:

- Narrator
- Maiba
- A mouse
- A frog
- An old woman
- Extras – Villagers

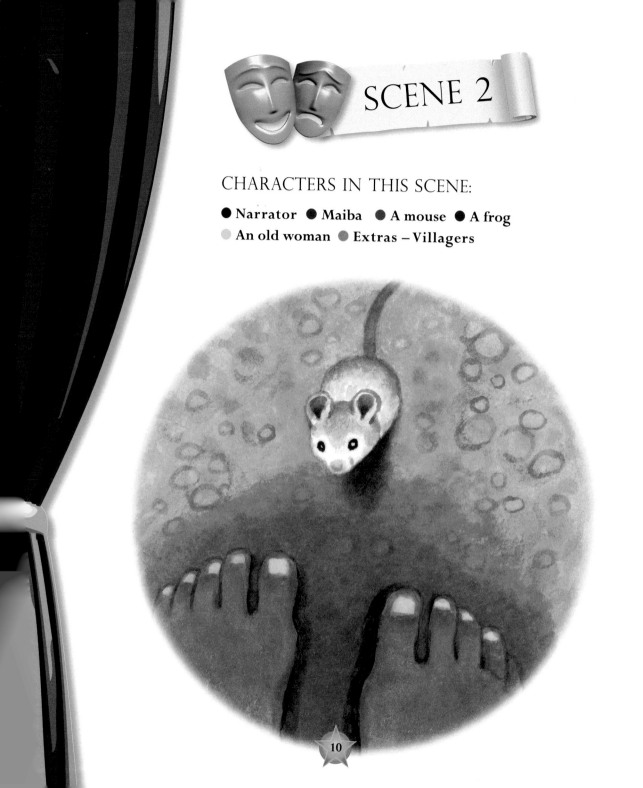

Maiba sets off along the path that will lead to the next village. She walks proudly with her head held high as the villagers and her family wave goodbye.

● **Narrator:** The very next morning, Maiba sets off on her journey. She is confident that it won't be long until she is the wife of the Great Chief.

● **Villagers:** Good luck, Maiba, travel safely!

A little while later, Maiba spots a mouse at the edge of the road.

● **Mouse:** *(looking up at Maiba)* Do you need me to show you the way to the village?

Maiba waves her hand dismissively at the little mouse.

● **Maiba:** I do not need your help. Now *(shouting)* GO!

● **Mouse:** *(warningly)* If you are unkind to all those that try to help you, you will fail.

● **Maiba:** You are not worthy to speak to me. I shall soon be the wife of the Great Chief. Leave me alone.

The mouse runs away in fright.

● **Narrator:** Maiba continues to travel on once more and before long she sees a frog in the middle of the path.

*Enter the **frog**.*

● **Frog:** Shall I show you the way to the next village? For it is hard to find with all the twists and turns in this path.

● **Maiba:** *(angrily)* Get away from me you slimy frog! How dare you speak to ME!

Maiba *runs past the **frog**, looking at him in disgust.*

● **Narrator:** Once more Maiba journeys onwards. When she stops to eat some bread, she meets an old begging woman sitting at the edge of the road.

● **Old woman:** *(holding out her hand to **Maiba**)* Might you have a spare crumb of bread to feed a hungry old woman?

● **Maiba:** *(knocking the **old woman**'s hand away)* No, I do not, you flithy old woman. Get away from me.

● **Old woman:** *(speaking gently)* Listen carefully, child. You must not always be so cruel for misfortune awaits you. You will soon see some trees that will laugh at you but you must not laugh in return. You will see a jug of milk but you must not drink from it.

Maiba: I won't listen to you. I do not need advice from an ugly, old woman! Now, go away!

Old woman: You have been warned…

SCENE 3

CHARACTERS IN THIS SCENE:

● **Narrator** ● **Maiba** ● **A young girl** ● **Extras –**
A chorus of trees, washer-women and villagers

Maiba reaches the forest and sees the river. The afternoon sun is beginning to set over the glistening water.

● **Narrator:** Before long, Maiba reaches a forest of trees. Just as the old woman had warned, the trees begin to laugh at her.

● **Chorus of trees:** Ha, ha, ha, ha, ha!

● **Maiba:** (*laughing back at the trees*) Ha, ha, ha! Oh, how funny! Laughing trees, whoever saw such a thing before!

● **Narrator:** But Maiba quickly thinks no more of the trees when she spots a jug of milk beside a tree trunk. She is thirsty from her long journey and drinks it all in one go. As Maiba wipes her mouth, she sees a group of washer-women at the edge of the river. One young girl looks up and waves to Maiba.

● **Young girl:** Where are you going, Sister? Might we help and show you the way to your destination?

● **Washer-women:** Yes, we would be pleased to help you, Child. Where do you travel to?

● **Maiba:** *(speaking angrily)* Stop asking me questions! How dare you call me your sister and child. You are nothing to me. I will soon be the wife of a Great Chief.

*Maiba crosses the river away from the **washer-women** and they watch sadly as she walks away without looking back.*

● **Narrator:** Eventually, Maiba reaches the Great Chief's village. She speaks to the villagers and tells them that she has come to meet their chief.

*Maiba enters the village as the **villagers** come to greet her.*

● **A villager:** You must be careful, for the chief is a clever man. He will not want a foolish wife. We suggest you make him a meal ready for his return at sunset.

*The **villagers** show **Maiba** into the **Great Chief**'s hut.*

SCENE 4

CHARACTERS IN THIS SCENE:

● **Narrator** ● **Maiba** ● **Great Chief** – wearing the mask of a snake with five heads ● **Extras** – Villagers and the wind

● **Narrator:** Maiba has prepared the Chief's meal and is waiting for his return. The sun has almost set.

● **Maiba:** (*talking to herself*) It's getting late. I have ground the grain and made the bread but where is the Great Chief?

● **Narrator:** Just then a strong wind starts to blow.

● **The wind:** Wooo, woooo, wooo, WOOOO!

● **Narrator:** The Great Chief enters his hut. He is a man with the heads of five snakes. Ten pairs of snake eyes glare angrily back at Maiba.

● **Maiba:** (*screaming in fright, covers her eyes*)
You hideous creature! What are you?

● **Great Chief:** (*gravely*) I am the Great Chief
but you will **never** be my wife. I know that you have
been cruel, proud and unkind to those that have tried to
help you. I will have no wife who behaves in such a way.
Return to your village at once!

*And, with that, **Maiba** flees the villlage in fear.*

SCENE 5

CHARACTERS IN THIS SCENE:

● **Narrator** ● **Sundai** ● **Rufaro** ● **Maiba**
● **Daya** ● **Extras – The villagers**

*Sundai, **Rufaro** and **Daya** are in the hut, listening to **Maiba**'s telling of what has come to pass. She is weeping as she tells her father all that has happened.*

● **Narrator:** Upon Maiba's return her father is very disappointed. He worries that his daughter has upset the Great Chief and ruined the family's chances of being linked to such an important village. Daya, upon seeing her father's distress, is keen to make her father happy once again.

Daya: Father, may I go to the village and try to please the Great Chief?

Rufaro: *(looking anxiously between **Sundai** and **Daya**)* Are you sure, Daya? Sundai, we have surely upset the Chief greatly. Might it be wise to leave the Great Chief alone and not anger him further?

Maiba: *(suddenly cries out)* The Great Chief is a hateful, ugly creature. You'll not want him as a husband, believe me!

Villagers: *(laughing as one **villager** speaks to the rest)* He, he, he! It sounds like the Great Chief showed her what kind of wife he doesn't want! Daya will be much better suited.

21

Sundai: *(smiling at **Daya**)* I do not fear the Great Chief's anger, for he is a fair and decent man, kind to his village and to all those he meets. In return, Daya is a sweet girl, Rufaro. I truly believe she'll make the Great Chief a wonderful wife.

Daya: *(standing and kissing **Sundai**'s cheek)* Thank you, Father. Please will you gather a bridal party for me, for I wish to show the Chief how proud I am of the village I come from.

Rufaro: Yes, Sundai, we must do it right this time.

Sundai: I agree. I will gather a party immediately, for no time must be lost.

*Sundai steps out into the village square and addresses the **villagers**.*

Sundai: Everyone, listen to me. I need to send my daughter to the Great Chief with the best bridal party he has ever seen. Who will help me?

Villagers: We will help! We will help!

*Very soon a large crowd of **villagers** has gathered to travel with **Daya** to meet the **Great Chief**.*

SCENE 6

CHARACTERS IN THIS SCENE:

- **Narrator**   - **An old woman**   - **A mouse**   - **A frog**
- **Daya**   - **A young girl**   - **Extras – The bridal party**

Daya *is travelling along the path to the next village with her large* **bridal party**.

- **Narrator:** Daya sets off to meet the Great Chief. As her sister before her, Daya meets the mouse.

- **Mouse:** Can I help you find your way to the village?

- **Daya:** *(smiles kindly and bends down to speak to the mouse)* Yes please, for I am sure to lose my way.

- **Mouse:** You must follow the road you are travelling on until you reach a large stone. From there, take the left path.

- **Narrator:** Daya thanks the mouse and follows the path he has shown her.

*She soon meets the same **frog** her sister met, sitting in the middle of the path, waiting for her. **Daya** gently picks up the frog.*

● **Frog:** Can I show you the way to the next village? For there are many twists and turns in this path.

● **Daya:** Thank you. I would be most grateful for your help. It is getting late and I wish to reach the village before sunset.

● **Frog:** The quickest way is through the trees up ahead. Once you see the river, the village is on the other side.

● **Daya:** You are very kind. Thank you.

*Daya puts the **frog** back down and continues on her way.*

Daya continues along the path and soon sees a row of trees in the distance.

● **Narrator:** At the edge of the forest, Daya meets an old beggar woman. Daya gives the frail woman her last loaf of bread. *(Hands over a loaf of bread.)*

● **Old woman:** Thank you for your kindness, Child. In return I shall offer you some advice. When you see a young girl by the river, take care to speak to her kindly.

● **Bridal party:** Come along Daya, we must hurry. We must reach the village by nightfall.

● **Daya:** *(turning to the **bridal party**)* Just a moment, please. *(to the **old woman**)* Thank you for your advice. I will do all that you advise.

Sure enough, **Daya** soon sees the **young girl** by the water's edge.

● **Young girl:** Where are you going to, Sister?

● **Daya:** *(smiling)* My journey has reached its end. I am here to see the Great Chief in the village just across this river.

● **Young Girl:** *(looks at **Daya** gravely)* When you meet him will you be afraid and look away from his face?

● **Bridal party:** (*scoffing*) Daya is too good and kind to be afraid of anyone's appearance.

● **Daya:** (*steadily returns the **young girl**'s gaze*) I promise I will look him directly in the eyes.

● **Young Girl:** I believe you. (*gives **Daya** some bread and meat from her basket*) Now take this food and prepare a meal for the Great Chief's return this evening. His hut is just across the river. Go now and get ready.

SCENE 7

CHARACTERS IN THIS SCENE:

● **Narrator** ● **Daya** ● **Great Chief**
● **Extras – Villagers and the wind**

● **Narrator:** Daya prepares and cooks a meal while she waits for the Great Chief. A strong wind can soon be heard and the Great Chief, masked as a five-headed snake, enters the hut.

● **The wind:** Wooo, woooo, woooo, WOOOO!

*Daya looks at the **Great Chief**.*

● **Narrator:** Bravely, Daya looks at the Chief's five snake heads and into his many piercing yellow eyes. She is afraid but is determined to keep her promise to the young girl at the river and will not look away in fear.

● **Daya:** Good evening, Chief. I have prepared your evening meal. I hope you enjoy it for I have worked hard all evening.

*The **Great Chief** sits down to eat his meal. Pause whilst he eats.*

● **Great Chief:** (*smiling at* **Daya**) Your food is delicious, Daya, thank you. More importantly, I know you are a kind and caring girl.

● **Daya:** (*looks him directly in the eyes*) May I ask, how could you know that?

● **Great Chief:** It was I who was the mouse, the frog and the old woman. I was even the young girl washing clothes in the river. I have seen how kind and generous you are. Please say you will be my wife?

The **Great Chief** *removes his mask and reveals the true man he is.*

● **Daya:** (*smiling*) I will, for I know we will be very happy.

● **Villagers:** (*cheering and clapping*) The Chief has found a wife!

● **Narrator:** And Daya was right. With each year that passed, the Great Chief loved his wife all the more. In return, Daya was the best wife she could be. But more importantly she remained as kind and true to all those she met as the day she left her home to become the Chief's bride.

The End

There are lots of websites you can visit to find out about Africa. Here are a few good places to begin:

CBBC: http://news.bbc.co.uk/cbbcnews/hi/static/find_out/specials/newsround_extra/africa/html/default.stm
Find out all about Africa, its people and its cultures.

More African Tales: http://africa.mrdonn.org/fables.html
If you enjoyed reading this folktale, find more on this website.

First published in 2015 by Wayland

Copyright © Wayland 2015

Wayland
An imprint of
Hachette Children's Group
Part of Hodder & Stoughton
Carmelite House
50 Victoria Embankment
London EC4Y 0DZ

Editor: Katie Woolley
Designer: Elaine Wilkinson
Illustrator: Adrienne Kennaway

Dewey Number: 822.9'2-dc22

ISBN: 978 0 7502 9708 0

10 9 8 7 6 5 4 3 2 1

Printed in China

An Hachette UK company.
www.hachette.co.uk
www.hachettechildrens.co.uk